WHY HUMANS WORK

How Jobs Shape Our Lives and Our World

ORCA
Think

Question, connect and take action to become better citizens
with a brighter future. Now that's smart thinking!

WHY HUMANS WORK

How Jobs Shape Our Lives and Our World

Monique Polak

illustrated by **Suharu Ogawa**

ORCA BOOK PUBLISHERS

Published in Canada and the United States in 2022 by Orca Book Publishers.
orcabook.com

Library and Archives Canada Cataloguing in Publication
Title: Why humans work : how jobs shape our lives and our world /
Monique Polak ; illustrated by Suharu Ogawa.
Names: Polak, Monique, author. | Ogawa, Suharu, 1979- illustrator.
Series: Orca think ; 6.
Description: Series statement: Orca think ; 6 | Includes bibliographical references and index.
Identifiers: Canadiana (print) 20210254327 | Canadiana (ebook) 20210254416 |
ISBN 9781459827950 (hardcover) | ISBN 9781459827967 (PDF) | ISBN 9781459827974 (EPUB)
Subjects: LCSH: Work—Juvenile literature. | LCSH: Labor—Juvenile literature. |
LCSH: Occupations—Juvenile literature. | LCSH: Work—Philosophy—Juvenile literature. |
LCSH: Work—Psychological aspects—Juvenile literature. | LCSH: Job satisfaction—Juvenile literature.
Classification: LCC HD4902.5 .P65 2022 | DDC j331—dc23

Library of Congress Control Number: 2021941166

Summary: Part of the nonfiction Orca Think series for middle-grade readers, this illustrated book explores
why we work and why people around the world end up in the jobs, careers and professions they do.

Orca Book Publishers is committed to reducing the consumption of nonrenewable resources in the
production of our books. We make every effort to use materials that support a sustainable future.

Orca Book Publishers gratefully acknowledges the support for its publishing programs provided
by the following agencies: the Government of Canada, the Canada Council for the Arts and the
Province of British Columbia through the BC Arts Council and the Book Publishing Tax Credit.

Cover and interior artwork by Suharu Ogawa
Design by Rachel Page
Layout by Dahlia Yuen
Edited by Kirstie Hudson

Printed and bound in Canada.

25 24 23 22 • 1 2 3 4

This book is dedicated to the students I taught at Marianopolis College during the COVID-19 pandemic. Thanks for working hard and helping me become an online teacher. Thanks for the sacrifices you made to keep others safe. May you lead happy, interesting lives and find work that makes this world a little better.

Contents

Introduction

"What do you want to be when you grow up?"

You've probably been asked that question.

When I was growing up in the 1960s, most kids came up with pretty much the same answers. Girls wanted to be nurses or teachers. Boys wanted to be firemen, doctors, lawyers or astronauts.

Today kids have many more options. You can be practically anything you want to be!

Over a lifetime, it is estimated that the average person will spend 90,000 hours at *work*—about a quarter of their lives!

Some people adore their work. My dad, who was a Quebec Court judge, enjoyed his *job* so much that he kept working until the age of 84! Others feel stuck in jobs they dislike. They can't wait to retire.

We must also remember that even in today's world, there are children, especially in developing countries, who are

Kids today have many options when it comes to a future career, like becoming a pro BMX racer!
THOMAS BARWICK/GETTY IMAGES

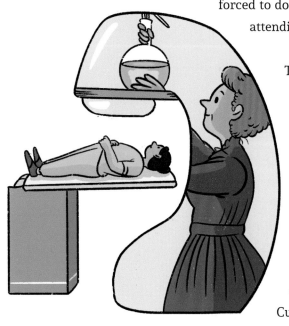

forced to do hard work and do not have the privilege of attending school.

Work changes our lives—and our world. The Egyptian pyramids were built by slaves, whose hard labor went unpaid. Thanks to the work of Orville and Wilbur Wright, we can travel by airplane. What most people don't know is that the Wright brothers got their start by opening a bicycle shop in Dayton, Ohio. As for the field of atomic physics, it would not exist were it not for Polish-French scientist Marie Curie, who toiled long hours in her laboratory developing the theory of **radioactivity**. It was also Curie who discovered that radiation could be used to treat cancerous tumors.

Work is rarely easy. That's why it's called work! Yet some people are paid to play—think trapeze artists and professional hockey players. But don't be fooled. To succeed, these people put in a lot of hard work.

Humans generally earn money for our work, though we may choose to do **volunteer work** for the satisfaction that comes from helping others.

Some jobs require little or no training. A job can be part-time or full-time, short- or long-term. A job is different from a **career**, a long-term professional journey that generally requires a certain level of education and training. But no matter what they do, most workers learn a great deal on the job. Sometimes those lessons are unexpected.

How we spend those 90,000 hours of work has a profound effect on our lives. Some people are **workaholics**, whose jobs interfere with their ability to enjoy life fully. Others strive for a balance between work and life.

It's clear that doing volunteer work makes this girl happy.

SDI PRODUCTIONS/GETTY IMAGES

IT STARTS WITH HOMEWORK

You probably first heard the word *work* in the second part of a compound word that most kids dislike—**homework**. But in some ways, homework trains us for the working world. Homework can be hard, and you would probably rather be playing outside or reading a book just for the fun of it. But, like it or not, homework has to get done.

Work has changed over the years. Long ago there was no distinction between work and everyday life. People just did what needed doing. They tended the land, sewed their own clothes and cooked their own food. Over time jobs became more specialized. Then, with the advent of the **Industrial Revolution**, new jobs were created. Computers also changed the working world. Most kids today rarely see a bank teller. That job has been largely replaced by ATMs (automated teller machines).

One thing we can be sure of is that the world of work will keep changing. While I was writing this book, our planet was struck by the COVID-19 pandemic, which, in addition to causing many deaths, left many people out of work and forced others to work from home. The pandemic led many of us to rethink our relationship with work. I'm one of the lucky people who was able to keep working during the pandemic. For me, work has a steadying effect during challenging times.

We can expect new jobs to arise in the next 30 years. Telesurgeons may perform surgeries using robotic tools, garbage designers will seek creative ways to help us dispose of waste, and aquaponic fish farmers will combine fish farming with gardening.

What do *you* want to be when you grow up?

Here's hoping this book will get you thinking about work—and play—and how the work you do will change your life and our world.

One
WORK VERSUS PLAY

A YOUNG KID'S JOB IS TO PLAY

A job is a task or regular activity that requires physical and mental energy and is generally performed in exchange for payment.

I have two jobs. I am a kids'-book writer and a teacher.

Most young children do not work. Their *job* (if you can call it a job—it certainly requires physical and mental energy) is to play.

How many times have your parents said to you, "Go to your room and play?" How many times have you rung the kid next door's doorbell and asked, "Can *so-and-so* (add your neighbor's name here) come out to play?" See what I mean? Little kids spend most of their waking hours playing. When they go to daycare and later preschool, there will be playtime there too.

Play begins almost as soon as a child is born. Babies enjoy a round of peekaboo, giggling to show their happiness.

> **"Choose a job you love, and you will never have to work a day in your life."**
> —Confucius, Chinese philosopher, 551–479 BCE

Even babies enjoy playing peekaboo.
CREATIVA IMAGES/SHUTTERSTOCK.COM

Toddlers play with blocks. And though there are hundreds of thousands of toys on the market, most kids can make do with simple stuff. Pots and pans make great toys. Clanging on them with a wooden spoon makes music. Several kids clanging together makes a band. And pots and pans can also be used for pretend cooking.

But play isn't only about having fun. Child psychologist Jean Piaget believed that play not only provides pleasure but is also connected to the development of children's intelligence.

Play also helps prepare you for your future life. Playing alone fosters independence. Playing with others—think board games and team sports—teaches cooperation, team-work and healthy rivalry. Pretending is educational too. It lets you try out new roles and experiences and see which ones you like. Here's a question for you. When you were little, what did you like pretending to be? Your answer may provide a clue about the kind of work you might enjoy doing one day.

When I was little, I played school in the basement of our house in Montreal. My students were my younger sister and various neighbors. When they were not available, I put our stuffed animals on chairs and taught them instead. Playing school showed me I liked being a teacher.

IN THE WORKS

Many adults forget how to play. Maybe it's because they are so busy doing grown-up things like working, raising families and paying bills that play rarely makes it on to their to-do lists. Adults who make time to play are more productive, more creative and happier than those who do not. Engaging in play reduces cortisol, the hormone associated with stress. Adults who play are healthier and have a reduced incidence of **dementia**. If you visit the Google campus in San Francisco, you will see ping-pong, billiards and foosball tables. Google not only wants to keep its employees happy and relaxed, but also understands that play increases productivity.

Playing reminds adults of childhood and can make them feel younger. Adults who feel younger than they really are turn out to be better workers. In a 2015 article published in the *Journal of Applied Psychology*, researchers at Germany's University of Konstanz studied 15,000 employees at 107 German companies. The research team found that employees who felt younger than their real ages accomplished more during the workday.

Homework helps kids learn.
FG TRADE/GETTY IMAGES

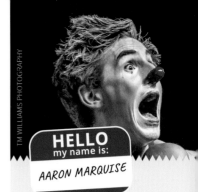

HELLO
my name is:
AARON MARQUISE

HOMEWORK: AN INTRODUCTION TO WORK

As kids grow up, there is less time for play. Most schools assign homework. Though homework is rarely fun, it is generally considered an important part of how kids learn. For many youngsters, having homework means their lives are getting more serious. Handing homework in on time teaches kids about responsibility and meeting deadlines.

In the grown-up world, most jobs involve work. Work can be mental or physical and sometimes both. When we're on the job, English teachers do more thinking than moving around. We spend many hours preparing for class and correcting assignments. A mechanical engineer designing a bridge puts in a lot of time working on plans.

Other jobs require physical labor. Construction workers, house painters and the man who shovels my front steps on a blizzardy day all exert a great deal of physical effort to get their jobs done.

ALL IN A DAY'S WORK

When, at the age of 20, Aaron Marquise told his parents he wanted to study clowning at Montreal's National Circus School his dad freaked out. "But he came around because I put the hard work in and showed him I could be successful," said Marquise.

Since he was a kid, Marquise wanted to be a performer. "I chose clowning because I love making people laugh. And I wanted to be able to play for a living," he told me.

Marquise is quick to add that being a clown takes a lot of hard work. Clowns do more than wear red noses and pull gags. He writes his own material. The clown characters he plays have their own unique personalities and back stories. Then come months of rehearsal. He spent a year preparing for his solo show *Oh, Garçon!* "It was exhausting," he recalled. "There were days in rehearsal when I couldn't think anymore."

These days, Marquise works in Troy, New York, as executive director of the Contemporary Circus and Immersive Arts Center. It's the perfect job for him. He gets to perform and also be in charge of what's happening onstage.

PLAYING FOR A LIVING

Of course, some people, like professional athletes and circus performers, are paid to play. From the outside, their jobs may look pretty perfect. But these people work hard too.

If you want to be a professional hockey player, you can't just lie on the couch and dream about playing in the national league. You need to lace up and head for the arena! Canadian hockey great Wayne Gretzky learned to skate on a rink his father built in the family's backyard in Brantford, Ontario. By the time he was six, Gretzky was playing hockey with the older boys in his neighborhood.

Dreaming about your future career—whether it's playing hockey, operating a crane, being an air-traffic controller or a doctor—has value too. These daydreams may also help you figure out what you want to do one day.

If you are lucky, your job may feel—at least sometimes—like play. Professional chefs work hard in their kitchens, but when they invent new recipes or joke around with colleagues and customers, their jobs can feel like play.

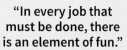

"In every job that must be done, there is an element of fun."

—Mary Poppins in the 1964 Disney movie *Mary Poppins*

Mary Poppins believed in the value of fun.

HANNAH PETERS/GETTY IMAGES

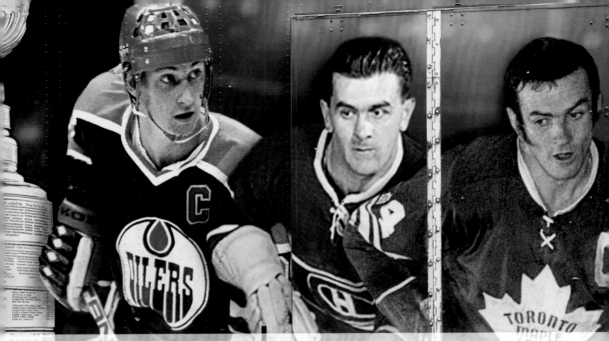

Canadian hockey great Wayne Gretzky learned to skate on a rink his father built in the family's backyard in Brantford, ON.
MEUNIERD/SHUTTERSTOCK.COM

These boys play street hockey. Perhaps they'll become professional hockey players someday too.
DAVID MADISON/GETTY IMAGES

WORK IN PROGRESS:
Is Hockey Only for Rich Kids?

Sometimes play costs a lot of money. Many people worry that hockey has become an elite sport for rich kids only. Consider that basic hockey gear—good-quality skates, sticks, a helmet, protective pads, a hockey jersey—costs at least $1,000. Then there are registration fees, travel costs, fees for private coaches, power skating camps and hockey academies. One year at the Canadian International Hockey Academy costs a whopping $53,000!

Wayne Gretzky worries about the exorbitant costs associated with playing hockey. If Gretzky were growing up today, his parents would not be able to afford to let him play hockey. "My parents couldn't afford it back when I was a kid," Gretzky said. "I remember being at a gas station… you'd stop to get gas and you could get two sticks for $1.99. My dad would buy me two sticks because that's what I'd use for the next three months."

Professional athletes like Gretzky earn a lot of money. In the 2017–2018 season, the average NHL salary was $2.78 million!

Organizations like the National Hockey League Players' Association are committed to making hockey accessible to all kids, regardless of their families' income. The organization has donated $22 million to hockey programs in 33 countries.

Two
THE HISTORY OF WORK

LIFE BEFORE JOBS

Modern humans have been around for about 130,000 years. For most of that time, there was no such thing as having a job as we know it today. Early humans simply did what had to get done—and there was plenty to do! As for children, they helped as soon as they were able to.

Our ancestors spent their days building fires to keep warm, making weapons, such as spears for hunting, and making their own clothing from animal skins. There was little free time to dream about playing sports or board games. No wonder that with so much work to do, early humans did not live long. During the Old Stone Age (also known as the Paleolithic period), average life expectancy was only 33 years.

SLAVERY: A TERRIBLE TRUTH

We cannot talk about the history of work without discussing *slave labor*—hard work for which people are paid little

IN THE WORKS

It has long been assumed that during the Old Stone Age, tasks were divided by gender, with women gathering fruits and vegetables to eat and looking after the children, and men doing the hunting. But new research shows our ancestors may not have been sexist after all. In a study reported on in the journal *Science*, anthropologists discovered that in at least some prehistoric societies, men and women shared tasks equally. Genealogical data collected from a hunter-gatherer population in the Philippines indicates that women not only collected honey, but also went hunting.

The Unsung Founders Memorial by artist Do-Ho Suh, at the University of North Carolina, honors the People of Color who helped build Carolina.
KELLEY L ALBERT/DREAMSTIME.COM

The invention of steam engines—this one is now part of the collection of the Deutsches Museum in Munich—heralded the start of the Industrial Revolution.
HEL080808/DREAMSTIME.COM

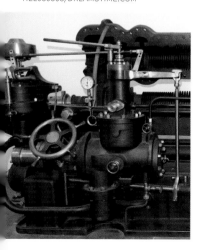

or nothing. Slavery has existed since the dawn of civilization. During the 17th and 18th centuries, Africans were kidnapped and forced to work as slaves in the Americas. In Canada, Indigenous and Black people were also forced into slavery before it was abolished in 1834. Though American president Abraham Lincoln's Emancipation Proclamation freed three million enslaved people in 1862, slavery continued in the United States until 1865.

Slavery is now illegal, but the terrible truth is that there are still slaves—and many modern slaves are children. (You will learn more about their plight in chapter three.)

THE INDUSTRIAL REVOLUTION CHANGES THINGS UP

The Industrial Revolution, which began in Britain and occurred from the late 18th to early 19th centuries, transformed the world of work. The invention of the steam engine is often seen as having ushered in the Industrial Revolution. Steam power led to the development of industries such as flour, paper and cotton mills, distilleries and waterworks. Employees were needed to operate all this new machinery.

With the Industrial Revolution, people began moving away from farmlands, and modern cities were born. Since men often continued to work the farms, many of the first people to move to cities were women.

Factories ran around the clock. It was not unusual for employees to work 10- to 16-hour days, seven days a week! In the 19th century, some British factories came up with a radical plan. They decided to give their workers half a day off on Saturday. However, the factory owners insisted workers had to be sober when they turned up for work the next morning!

LOOKING OUT FOR WORKERS

The **labor movement** arose to improve working conditions and living standards. Fed up with their long hours, dangerous working conditions and poor pay, workers banded together to form **trade unions**. It took the labor movement decades to get workers a full day off on Saturdays. It was not until 1908 that a New England textile mill agreed to give employees a five-day week. Thirty years later, in 1938, the Fair Labor Standards Act gave Americans the modern 40-hour five-day workweek.

> "Every moment is an organizing opportunity, every person a potential activist, every minute a chance to change the world."
>
> —Dolores Huerta, American labor leader and cofounder of the National Farmworkers Association, born 1930

> "Fight for the things you care about, but do it in a way that will lead others to join you."
>
> —Ruth Bader Ginsburg, Associate Justice of the Supreme Court of the United States, 1933–2020

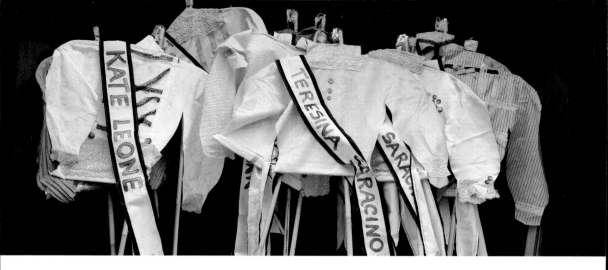

The 104th anniversary of the tragic Triangle Shirtwaist Factory fire was observed at the factory's former site.

A KATZ/SHUTTERSTOCK.COM

It sometimes takes a tragedy before conditions improve. In 1911 a fire broke out at the Triangle Shirtwaist Factory in New York City's Greenwich Village. One hundred and forty-six garment workers died in the fire. Of those who perished, 123 were girls, some as young as 14, and women. Most of the victims were Italian or Jewish immigrants from eastern Europe. What made the fire so deadly was that the building's exits and the doors to the stairwells had all been locked, partly to prevent theft, but mostly so workers could not take unauthorized coffee breaks. That fire led to the growth of the International Ladies' Garment Workers' Union—and to improved safety standards in workplaces around the world.

In Africa agriculture is the largest economic sector. Many Africans do backbreaking work for little pay.

ANDRE SILVA PINTO/SHUTTERSTOCK.COM

Not all regions of the world, however, experienced or benefited from the Industrial Revolution. The terms **developed world** and **developing world** are used to distinguish between countries with industrialized economies and those with low- to middle-income economies, where there has been less industrialization. In Africa, for example, the largest economic sector today is farming, which means backbreaking work for little pay. People in developing nations have less access to things that many of us in the developed world take for granted, such as safe water, education and libraries.

HELLO
my name is:
JOHN DAVIDSON

ALL IN A DAY'S WORK

In 2016 John Davidson retired at the age of 63, after a 30-year career as a milkman in Tulsa, Oklahoma. Davidson used to get up at 4:00 a.m. so he could deliver his customers' milk on time. Customers trusted him so much that some even gave him the keys to their houses. At one time he had nearly 300 customers. That number had dropped to about 70 by 2016.

What he loved most about his job as a milkman was his connection with his customers. "Everyone was happy to see me when I showed up. They appreciated me. The kids loved me," he said. It probably helped that he brought his dog, Sam, on the morning milk run. "I had one customer on Tuesday mornings who had a tennis ball for Sam. And she'd always make me a coffee," he told me.

It was Davidson's family who insisted he retire. Delivering milk was hard on his back, and his family worried about his health. But no one wanted to take over his business and buy his milk route. "It's hard to get new customers. I think it's because people don't want strangers around at their houses," he said.

So far, retirement also suits Davidson. There's time for fishing with his grandchildren, and he does chores for neighbors. "But," he told me, "I'll always be a milkman. My wife and I drink two and a half gallons of milk a week. Maybe I live in the past. I like the way things used to be done. You got more personal contact."

WORK IN PROGRESS: *Who Doesn't Love a Three-Day Weekend?*

Before she was elected Finland's prime minister in 2019, Sanna Marin proposed that Finland adopt a four-day workweek. The country believes in flexible work schedules. Since 1996 the Finns have been legally entitled to come in earlier or stay later at work by up to three hours. That flexibility has reportedly made Finnish workers happier—and more productive. Companies around the world are paying attention to these changes. In the summer of 2019, Microsoft Japan implemented a four-day workweek for its employees. The company reported that the change led to a 40 percent increase in its employees' productivity. The new schedule was especially popular with younger workers.

MON   WED   FRI   SUN

TUE   THU   SAT

Many of today's kids are accustomed to working on computers.

TUAN TRAN/GETTY IMAGES

COMPUTERS ARRIVE ON THE SCENE

Though computers have been around since the 1950s, it was not until the 1980s that they became widely used by the general public. Thanks to computers, paperwork became easier and more efficient—and it required way less paper. Files could be stored virtually instead of in filing cabinets. Thanks to email, employees could communicate instantly. Some meetings no longer had to take place in person. Instead, people in different countries could meet up using computer applications such as Zoom.

Working remotely, a term that refers to working from home (or from a coffee shop down the street), became more common once personal computers hit the scene in the late 1970s and early 1980s. People who work remotely can choose their own hours, taking time off, for example, to take their children to school or pick them up at the end of the day. Many employees jump at the chance to work remotely.

But the arrival of computers was bad news for some businesses, like the printing business. Newspapers, magazines and books were once typeset on giant printing presses. Now all that is done on computers. People whose hands used to get inky running printing presses had to learn about computers in a hurry!

Computers also transformed the banking industry. When I was growing up in the 1960s, bank tellers recorded transactions using pen and paper. Today there are hardly any bank tellers. Many people use ATMs (automated teller machines) to withdraw and deposit money. Others prefer to do their banking online. The first ATM was used in London in 1967. Drive-through ATMs were introduced in the United States in 1980.

In some ways, the arrival of computers has us working harder than ever. Because many of us are always within reach of a computer or cell phone, colleagues and employers can reach us at any hour. Many of us find ourselves working well past 5:00 p.m.

Perhaps because of these factors, many people today strive for a better *work-life balance*. Some choose (or have no choice but) to work freelance, combining careers in what is known as the *gig economy*.

One thing we know for sure is that the world of work will keep changing.

Most bank tellers have been replaced by ATMs. And even ATMs are becoming less popular as more and more people are doing their banking online.

JOOS MIND/GETTY IMAGES

Minimum wage is the lowest wage permitted by law. Which countries have the highest minimum wage? If you guessed Luxembourg and Australia, you're right!

1. Luxembourg
2. Australia
3. France
4. New Zealand
5. Germany
6. Netherlands
7. Belgium
8. United Kingdom
9. Ireland
10. Canada

WORLDPOPULATIONREVIEW.COM

Three
KIDS
AT WORK
OVER TIME AND
AROUND THE WORLD

KIDS ARE HARD WORKERS

As we saw in chapter two, before there were jobs as we know them today, kids worked as soon as they were able to. Even a three-year-old would have helped find wood to build a fire, or pick berries for eating.

It's interesting, too, that when children engage in what is called pretend play, they sometimes pretend to be grown-ups in the working world. When we were little, my sister Carolyn and I played restaurant and jewelry store. But as I mentioned, my favorite pretend game was school.

Fast-forward to when I was being interviewed for my first job as a teaching assistant at Concordia University. The head of the writing program wanted to know if I had any teaching experience. "Of course I do!" I answered. "I taught in our basement for years!" Guess what? I got the job!

Some kids are paid for doing chores. Babysitting and mowing lawns are among the most common first jobs for

Kids can get paid for doing chores such as shoveling snow.
LIUBOVYASHKIR/DREAMSTIME.COM

many preteens and teenagers. First jobs teach kids responsibility—and are a way for kids to earn pocket money!

Some kids have more glamorous jobs. Take, for example, child actors like Marsai Martin, an American actor and producer who got her start at the age of 10 when she was cast in the ABC comedy series *Black-ish*. Young baseball fans dream of getting a job as a batboy or batgirl, the kid who lays out equipment and brings bats to members of a baseball team.

These teens work part-time in a café.
STURTI/GETTY IMAGES

IN THE WORKS

According to the Pew Research Center, in the late 1990s, 50 percent of American teens had summer jobs. But by the summer of 2018, only 34.6 percent of American teens were employed. Several factors help explain the drop in teen employment. Rather than working on weekends and over the summers the way so many teenagers used to, more and more teens who have the opportunity and the financial means to pursue postsecondary education are opting to spend their free time on activities they hope will boost their chances of getting into their first-choice college or university. That means doing volunteer work, taking extra courses and doing unpaid *internships*.

But working part-time—even if it means flipping burgers or reminding kids to shower before they get into the swimming pool—turns out to have important benefits beyond earning some extra cash. Teens who work part-time get a chance to "try out" a job and see whether they like it. They also learn about responsibility and managing their own money. According to the Center for Work Ethic Development, a Colorado-based organization, part-time jobs also teach young people *soft skills* such as getting along with others, communicating, leadership, teamwork and problem-solving.

This gondolier does his thing in the canals of Venice.
IMAGEBROKER.COM/SHUTTERSTOCK.COM

WHERE IN THE WORLD?

Geography can influence the kind of work children do or dream of doing. If your dream is to be a gondolier, you had better live in Venice, where gondoliers operate flat-bottomed boats called gondolas. If you can never have enough Parmesan cheese on your pasta, you might want to become a Parmigiano-Reggiano tester. These testers work in Italy too, where they tap wheels of cheese. They know from the sound whether the cheese is good enough to eat. If you enjoy pushing people around, you might apply for a job in Tokyo, where oshiya, or pushers, literally push people onto crowded trains. If you like ravens, consider a job at the Tower of London in England, the only place in the world that employs raven masters. These raven masters look after the resident ravens believed to protect the tower and the royal family.

Hou Han Zhang as a baby, pictured here with his grandfather Zhang Zu De. Zhang Zu De began working at the age of seven.

PHOTO COURTESY OF HOU HAN ZHANG

ALL IN A DAY'S WORK

Hou Han Zhang was my student at Marianopolis College. When I told my class I was researching **child labor**, Hou Han Zhang told me about his grandfather Zhang Zu De, who is now 90 and lives in China.

Zhang Zu De grew up in Bobai, a county in Guangxi, China. Because his family was poor, he began working at the age of seven, first as a helper at a food stand and, later, tending cows on a local farm. By the time he was eight, Zhang Zu De was working full-time in the rice fields.

He will never forget the time he was accidentally sprayed with a toxic chemical pesticide used on the rice in those days. "People thought he'd die," Hou Han Zhang told me. "Someone even told him, 'You don't have a lot of poops left to take.'" But to everyone's surprise, Zhang Zu De survived.

During the Chinese Cultural Revolution, Zhang Zu De was sent to work for the army. He did such a good job that when the revolution ended, the officer to whom he had been reporting arranged for him to attend school in Beijing. When he graduated, Zhang Zu De became vice mayor of Bobai, a position he held for three years.

THE MISTREATMENT OF CHILDREN IN THE WORKFORCE

The United Nations defines child labor as "work for which the child is either too young…or work which, because of its detrimental nature or conditions, is altogether considered unacceptable for children and is prohibited." In other words, child labor refers to the **exploitation** of child workers.

Unfortunately, there is a long history of mistreatment of children in the working world. After the Great Fire of London in 1666, building regulations were changed so chimneys would be more narrow and less likely to catch fire. The only people who could fit inside such narrow chimneys to clean them were six-year-old boys. These boys came from poor families who sold their sons to a master who made the boys work as sweeps. These sweeps were exposed to creosote, a dangerous chemical. If the children didn't work hard enough, they were forced down the chimneys with sticks. This practice continued for more than 200 years. It ended in 1875, after a boy named George Brewster became trapped in a chimney and died shortly after being freed.

Even in today's world, there are children who are forced to work long hours in harsh and sometimes terrible conditions. The International Labour Organization estimates that 170 million children are engaged in child labor. Though child labor is illegal in most countries, it remains common, especially in some of the poorest parts of the world.

In the fashion industry, children are used to pick cotton, spin yarn, dye fabric, assemble pieces of fabric and sew on buttons. In countries such as India, Bangladesh, Pakistan and China, many children work in **sweatshops**, factories with poor working conditions.

"You may not control all the events that happen to you, but you can decide not to be reduced by them."

—Maya Angelou, American poet, memoirist and activist, 1928–2014

WORK IN PROGRESS:
Five Industries in Which Child Labor Is Common

- Coffee production
- Cotton picking
- Brick production
- Sugarcane harvesting
- Gold mining

A child laborer at work in a Bangladeshi garment factory.

STEVENK/SHUTTERSTOCK.COM

> "We owe our children, the most vulnerable citizens in our society, a life free of violence and fear."
>
> —Nelson Mandela, former president of South Africa, 1918–2013

PROTECTING KIDS

Child trafficking is a serious crime that is widely reported in countries such as India, China, Pakistan and Cambodia. Trafficked children are recruited, kidnapped and forced to work as slaves. According to the International Labour Organization, more than one million children are trafficked every year.

In India, child trafficking is widespread. Children there, especially young girls from poor families, are often tricked by traffickers who offer them real jobs—for example, working as vendors at a market—only to force them to work as beggars, in factories or in the *sex trade*. Child trafficking happens in every corner of the world, including North America.

Karly Church is a crisis-intervention counselor with Victim Services of Durham Region, outside Toronto. She also works with the police, helping underage girls who have been lured into sex trafficking. Church is a survivor of sex trafficking. In a powerful TEDxOshawa talk, Church describes her experience. A runaway, Church was in her early twenties, living on the streets, when she was first trafficked.

"How," Church asks, "can we ignite change?" The answer, she says, is educating ourselves and others. Church thinks that if, when she was growing up, she had heard the kind of presentation she now gives to young people, if she had been aware of such warning signs as a man paying a lot of attention to her, giving her expensive gifts and isolating her from family and friends, she might not have been trafficked. But the harrowing experience she had as a young woman has made her an advocate for change—specifically the need to speak openly with young people about abuse of all kinds. For Church, protecting children is more than a job. It's a way of transforming a painful experience into something positive.

These girls are protesting the trafficking of children, reminding us that children (or any human beings) must never be treated as goods that are for sale.
NOAM GALAI/GETTY IMAGES

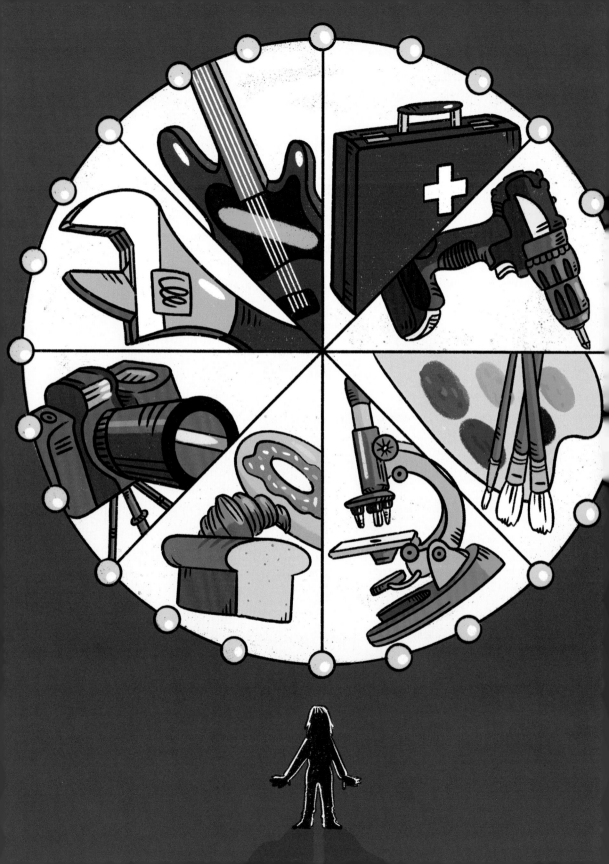

Four
DECISIONS, DECISIONS!
FINDING A JOB THAT'S RIGHT FOR YOU

NOT EVERYONE GETS TO CHOOSE

If you are privileged, you may get to choose your future job.

But not everyone is privileged.

Some children are born having no choice about the work they will do in the future. In India, a complicated *caste system*, believed to date back to 1000 BCE, determines what kind of work Hindu children will do once they are old enough to work. When a child is born, they automatically belong to one of four castes—Brahmins, Kshatriyas, Vaishyas or Shudras. Brahmins are at the top of the pyramid. Traditionally they have become priests or intellectuals. Kshatriyas are warriors or rulers. Vaishyas are traders or businesspeople. The Shudras, who are at the bottom of the pyramid, do menial jobs like cleaning the streets. And within the Shudras there is another hierarchy, with a group called Dalits at the very bottom. Dalit children do not get the opportunity to attend school, their families

> "We are all of us stars, and we deserve to twinkle."
> —Marilyn Monroe, actor, 1926–1962

HELLO
my name is:
GUY ROULEAU

ALL IN A DAY'S WORK

Guy Rouleau is the director of the Neuro (Montreal Neurological Institute-Hospital). Though Rouleau's father was a doctor, Rouleau never felt pressure to follow in his footsteps.

Rouleau, who grew up in Ottawa, was six or seven years old when he attended a science open house at the University of Ottawa. He remembers seeing a professor freeze liquid mercury using liquid nitrogen. "The mercury became as hard as steel. He even used it as a hammer to hammer nails. It was so fascinating," Rouleau said. That fascination with science led Rouleau to study medicine and do scientific research. Rouleau discovered the genetic basis of many brain diseases, including autism, amyotrophic lateral sclerosis (also known as Lou Gehrig's disease) and schizophrenia. Nearly 60 years after he first visited the University of Ottawa, Rouleau remains fascinated by science.

do not have access to running water, and their menial jobs pay less than two dollars a day. Though much effort has been made to do away with India's caste system, it continues to exist, especially in the country's small towns, where more than 70 percent of Indians live.

YOUR DREAM JOB

You may be surprised to learn that only about 10 percent of people end up doing the jobs they dreamed of doing when they were kids!

That is because many factors determine how people land in certain jobs. These factors include **happenstance**, geography, other people's expectations and, of course, opportunity and privilege. Not every child is able to attend college or university, and this can limit their job prospects. Other young people forego higher education because they need to work to support their families. In chapter six you will learn more about **equity** and **diversity** in the workplace, and how historically, and even today, some individuals have been and continue to be discriminated against.

THE ROLE OF HAPPENSTANCE

The word *happenstance* refers to random or chance events. It can be argued that to be born into a Brahmin or Dalit family is happenstance. There are lots of other, happier examples of happenstance—some might call it fate—leading people to a certain job or career.

Amanda Di Sensi never dreamed she would become a dog walker and business owner. When she was growing up, her plan was to become a lawyer or politician. But when Di Sensi did an internship at a legal firm, she discovered that practicing law was not for her. If, in 2014, Di Sensi had not moved to Nuns' Island—a Montreal community with lots of dog-friendly green space—she might never have fallen into the dog-walking business.

During her first week on Nuns' Island, Di Sensi spotted a woman walking several dogs. They chatted, and the woman offered Di Sensi a job as her assistant. A year later, Di Sensi took over the business. Today she has 75 canine clients—and her own assistant.

"I much prefer to work with animals than people," Di Sensi told me. "I never get yelled at."

Other people's expectations can also influence our job choices. Some people end up doing the jobs they were expected to do. Well-meaning family members, parents in particular, may have a plan for their children's futures. At the college where I teach, I have met many students enrolled in the Health Science program not because they love science, but because it was their parents' dream that their children become doctors.

> "The only way to do great work is to love what you do. If you haven't found it yet, keep looking. Don't settle."
>
> —Steve Jobs, cofounder of Apple Inc., 1955–2011

Amanda Di Sensi owns a dog-walking service. She says she prefers working with dogs over humans.

TOP: PHOTO COURTESY OF AMANDA DI SENSI
BOTTOM: HEDGEHOG94/SHUTTERSTOCK.COM

ALL IN THE FAMILY

Walmart was founded in 1962. Though the company went public in 1970, the Waltons remain the wealthiest family in the United States.

RICK T. WILKING/GETTY IMAGES

Three generations of one family stand outside their dry goods store in Malaysia.

XPACIFICA/GETTY IMAGES

Some families own businesses they hope younger family members will take over one day. A well-known example of a family business is Walmart, founded in 1962 by Sam Walton. Walmart went public in 1970, but Sam Walton's son Rob is still on the board of directors. The Waltons are the wealthiest family in the United States.

But there's bad news—only 3 percent of family businesses make it past the third generation. Many researchers have looked at the challenges associated with family businesses. When I was growing up, one of the largest grocery-store chains in Montreal was called Steinberg's, named for the family that owned it. If someone needed to buy tools or paint, they went to J. Pascal's Hardware and Furniture, owned by the Pascal family. Neither of those businesses made it past the third generation.

According to researchers, one of the main reasons family businesses tend to fail over time—or are sold off—is that often by the third generation, grandchildren are less interested in the family business than their grandparents were. Many of those grandparents scrimped and saved and worked long hours to establish their businesses. Though the grandchildren likely benefited from their grandparents' and parents' hard work, some may have little interest in the family business or in working as hard as their grandparents did.

Researchers have also found that family businesses fare better when subsequent generations can develop their own areas of expertise to help grow the business. Bigelow Tea, the top specialty tea seller in the United States, was founded in 1945 by Ruth Bigelow. Today it is run by Ruth's granddaughter Cindi, whose expertise in social media has helped the company increase online sales.

This girl is having fun working at a potter's wheel. Perhaps one day she will become a professional potter.

ANTONIODIAZ/SHUTTERSTOCK.COM

HOW TO CHOOSE?

Reinekke Lengelle thinks adults should not pressure children into feeling they have to come up with a right answer for their career choice. Lengelle, a professor at Athabasca University in Edmonton, whose specialties include helping students use writing to discover what she calls their "career identity," tries not to use the word *choice* when it comes to jobs or careers.

"Choosing is a big word in career learning," Lengelle told me. "It's too rational. What works better is spying on yourself to see what you are already doing—and to ask delicious questions."

HELLO
my name is:
RICKY BLITT

ALL IN A DAY'S WORK

Ricky Blitt is one of the original writers and directors of the animated sitcom *Family Guy*.

But when Blitt was a kid living in Montreal, he had no idea what he wanted to do when he grew up. He knew he could make people laugh. "It was the thing people complimented me for," he said.

Blitt studied communications at McGill University. Later he wrote a sample script for a CBC sitcom. On the basis of that script, he was hired to work on the show. That experience helped him get accepted to the American Film Institute in Los Angeles.

Looking back, Blitt says, "I went there before I was ready. I was a bit overwhelmed." Blitt dropped out after one semester and returned to Montreal. It would be nearly 10 years before Blitt returned to Los Angeles.

Blitt borrowed money from his parents and went back to Los Angeles with three scripts he had written. He didn't sell those scripts, but an agent asked him to write another script. That led to Blitt's being hired as a staff writer for a sitcom called *The Parent 'Hood*. Since then Blitt has never been out of work. "I had it wrong thinking in life you only get one shot at things. I learned it's impossible to fail at something if you try. As long as I try even a tiny bit, then my dreams are one step closer."

WORK IN PROGRESS:
Get Ready for Good Luck

Many people report that good luck played a role in their careers. But according to researchers Robert Pryor and Jim Bright, good luck isn't just a matter of…well…luck. Their research shows people need to be *ready* for good luck. The pair came up with a Luck Readiness Index, which identifies eight "dimensions" of good luck. Do you have the attitudes Pryor and Bright describe? If not, maybe you can work on developing them. Good luck!

- **Flexibility**—openness to change
- **Optimism**—ability to continue trying, even in a difficult situation
- **Risk [tolerance]**—confidence in your ability to make decisions in response to change
- **Curiosity**—desire for new knowledge and experiences
- **Persistence**—ability to endure boredom, frustration and sometimes disappointment
- **Strategy**—ability to seek out opportunities
- **Efficacy**—desire to take control of your life
- **Luckiness**—belief that good things will happen to you

This boy seems to be enjoying the job fair at his school.
SDI PRODUCTIONS/GETTY IMAGES

Back in the 1980s, when Lengelle was in high school, her guidance counselor gave her **aptitude tests**. These tests, common at the time, attempted to match personality traits with existing jobs. Based on the results of the test, Lengelle's guidance counselor recommended she become a scientist or astronaut. "Considering I get nauseous when I'm sitting in the back of a bus or car, I don't think I'd have made a very good astronaut," Lengelle told me.

Today, in part because we know that few people follow a clear, linear career path, aptitude tests have become a thing of the past. Nowadays high school guidance counselors take a more open-ended approach to help young people contemplate their future careers by organizing career fairs or career days. Visitors from different fields come to a school to describe the work they do and what education and skills were required to get where they are.

Sometimes the people kids meet at a career fair may go on to become **mentors** or positive role models who can also play an important role in helping young people determine the kind of work they might enjoy.

Lengelle believes that what young people need most in order to discover their "work identity" is the activation of what she calls "a warm inner compass." It's a kind of personal GPS device that checks our direction. The compass is warm because it connects us with the things that make us feel most alive. To Lengelle, a warm inner compass is the result of talking to—and listening to—ourselves. In our society we often look for an outside expert opinion. But when it comes to discovering your work identity, no outside expert can give you the answer. There's only one real expert—you! Lengelle is convinced that in order to discover your work identity, you need to trust yourself.

"What do you like?" and "What are you good at?" are two questions adults often ask kids trying to figure out what work they'd like to do.

Lengelle prefers less direct questions, such as "What kinds of books do you buy or take from the library?" "What kind of movies do you like?" "If you could do a master class online, who would you pick to teach it?" "What can't you stand?" and "Who was your childhood hero?"

No magic wand can help you decide on a job or career. The work you end up doing will depend on many factors, and only some of those will be under your control.

IN THE WORKS

Kids and teens are often told, "Follow your passion." But researchers at California's Stanford University have found this may not always be the best advice. What if, for example, you have many passions? What if there's nothing you feel particularly passionate about? But the main danger, according to the Stanford research team, is that people who follow their passion tend to expect they will always enjoy their work and that their work will feel easy. This attitude can backfire and actually cause people to give up too quickly.

The secret to success has more to do with effort than passion—though having a passion for something may lead us to put in more effort! Paul O'Keefe, the chief researcher behind the study, warns that "urging people to find their passion may lead them to put all their eggs in one basket, but then to drop that basket when it becomes difficult to carry."

Five
LEARNING
THE ROPES
TRAINING FOR A JOB

"GOT EXPERIENCE?"

If you're looking for a job, you'll probably be asked whether you have experience. Of course, when you're just starting out in the working world, your answer is likely to be no. How's a kid supposed to get experience if employers only want to hire experienced workers? Generations of preteens and teenagers have asked themselves this question!

Here's another question. Once you land a job, how do you learn the ropes?

Some people learn on the job, such as those who do **unskilled labor**, work that requires no special training. Schools can help prepare us for the working world. Certain jobs require a university degree. If you want to become, for example, a doctor, lawyer, engineer or accountant, you will need to complete specialized university studies. **Vocational schools**—job-training centers that give students hands-on practical experience in trades ranging from

This college student is well prepared for his interview and has printed out his résumé.
SDI PRODUCTIONS/GETTY IMAGES

hairdressing to plumbing—are another option. An unpaid or paid internship is also a way to get experience. Some people have mentors, experienced workers willing to pass on their knowledge to those who are just starting out.

Anyone can do unskilled labor. But some jobs requiring no special skills tend to be done more by males than females. (In chapter six we will learn more about how factors such as gender have limited people's work options.)

This young painter is doing volunteer work.
SOLSTOCK/GETTY IMAGES

LEARNING ON THE JOB

Kyle Gravel started working for 1-800-GOT-JUNK?— a Montreal junk-removal service—in the summer of 2018. Gravel, who is studying physics at Concordia University, learned about the job on a job-listing website. There was only one requirement. 1-800-GOT-JUNK? wanted bilingual employees, something that is especially important in the province of Quebec, where there are many French speakers. "It also helped that I had a driver's license," Gravel told me. For his job, Gravel drives around town in a company truck, collecting junk from people's houses or worksites and delivering it to the company's warehouse, where the junk is sorted. "We recycle everything," he said.

But even junk collecting requires some training. Employees always work with a partner. When Gravel started out, he was paired with a trainer named Costa, who had been with the company for six years. "He taught me how to lift a fridge without hurting myself," said Gravel. "You have to lift with your knees, not your back." These days Gravel trains other employees, including his friend Andrew Panton, who now works for the company too and is Gravel's regular partner.

Cameron Knowlton (you'll learn more about him in chapter eight) also does unskilled labor, working as a cashier and bagger at a Montreal grocery store. "I learned from hands-on experience," said Knowlton. Unlike Gravel, Knowlton did not have an official trainer, but he got useful tips from co-workers. "Here's one example. They showed me

During the summer, Kyle Gravel (that's him on the right, wearing a hat) and his pal Andrew Panton do a lot of heavy lifting for a Montreal junk-removal service.
PHOTO COURTESY OF MONIQUE POLAK

Engineering student Marc Zawi has a part-time job as a lead screener for the City of Montreal. He tests lead levels in Montrealers' water pipes.

PHOTO COURTESY OF MONIQUE POLAK

> "Think of ways you can give back— so you can help."
>
> —Ngoc-Diep Thi Vu, Vietnamese-born chemist, 1943–2019, advice to daughter Diane Bui when Diane was growing up

how to organize the returned beer bottles by sorting them according to brand and color," he explained. Something Knowlton has had to learn on the job is how to deal with difficult customers. "When items don't scan properly, they sometimes blame me. I've been sworn at once or twice. But I have a brick-wall demeanor. I have to remain professional and act like it doesn't mean anything, even when it does," he said.

Marc Zawi has two jobs. Zawi works as a replacement lab technician in pharmacies and a lead screener for the City of Montreal, testing lead levels in water pipes. He is also studying industrial engineering at Polytechnique Montréal. Zawi's first job was at a pet store back when he was 16. "I got fired after six months for often being one or two minutes late," he told me. But that, said Zawi, was the last time he was fired from a job. "Unless life gets in the way, I try to always be on time now," he said.

HIRE A PROFESSIONAL

Some jobs, known as *professions*, require university training —and, in many cases, internships. Once Canadian doctors graduate from medical school, they must do residencies, which range from two to seven years. Neurologist Guy Rouleau (you met him in chapter four) attended medical school at the University of Ottawa. After that he did his residency at McGill University. Then he went on to do a PhD in genetics at Harvard University. During the first two and a half years of medical school, Rouleau learned the theory of medicine. During the final year and a half, he was in the hospital as a student, doing what was then called a clerkship, learning at patients' bedsides from physician-teachers. "I learned how to approach a medical problem and how to solve and treat it," said Rouleau. To maintain his medical license, Rouleau must complete a certain number of hours of continuing medical education every year. In other words, he's still learning!

Diane Bui is a lawyer working in Washington, DC, for the United States Agency for International Development. After completing a bachelor of arts degree (often called a BA) in environmental science, Bui studied law at New York University. "I learned how to think and process questions like a lawyer—breaking issues down into their components and looking at the different angles," said Bui. But she learned on the job too. "I learned what my clients needed me to do in addition to answering their legal questions," she said. Bui worked for five years at a law firm before finding a job in international development—the field she'd always wanted to be in.

According to the National Center for Education Statistics, people with a BA earn nearly $17,000 a year more than those with only a high school diploma. But not everyone can or wants to attend university. Some people don't enjoy school. Others do not have the money to pay for tuition or cannot take time off from their paid jobs to return to school. For some, vocational school—also known as trade school—is the right choice.

At the New York University School of Law, Diane Bui trained to become a lawyer.

PHOTO COURTESY OF DIANE BUI

I thought Carissa Smith was alluding to the song "Little Drummer Boy" when she named her company Little Plumber Girl. But I was wrong. Smith is five feet, four inches (1.6 meters) tall. When she was an apprentice plumber, clients whose homes she worked at often wanted her back when they needed a plumber. It was not only because she had done a good job, but also because many customers liked the idea of hiring a female plumber. "Some of the clients were seniors living alone. They might find a huge, burly man intimidating. I'm small and not intimidating," she said. But some customers had trouble remembering Carissa's name. "So they'd call and ask, 'Can you send me the little plumber girl?'" The name stuck!

Some plumbers don't like customers who ask a lot of questions. But questions don't bother Smith. "I think people feel comfortable asking me questions," she said. Smith is also good at diagnosing problems. I asked Smith whether dealing with poop is the grossest part of her job. But I was wrong about that too. "Grease traps are the grossest thing. They have a really bad smell. I've seen some men plumbers vomit when they work on grease traps. But it's never happened to me," Smith said.

Customers used to call Carissa Smith "the little plumber girl." The term came in handy when she was looking for a name for her plumbing-services company.
PHOTO COURTESY OF CARISSA SMITH

VOCATIONAL TRAINING

Vocational schools offer training for specific jobs such as electrician, carpenter and dental hygienist. Class sizes tend to be small, and vocational training programs can usually be completed within nine months to two years.

Carissa Smith is a plumber who owns Little Plumber Girl, an Edmonton plumbing service. Smith challenges gender expectations, since plumbing—and the construction industry in general—is male-dominated. In 2010, only 1.5 percent of American plumbers were female. But that is changing. According to the National Association of Women in Construction, 9.9 percent of all those employed in the American construction sector in 2018 were female.

Smith grew up on a farm in Saskatchewan. Not long after graduating from high school, Smith went into the real estate business with her grandmother. Smith, who always liked hands-on work, did some of the painting and plumbing in the buildings she and her grandmother owned. That experience led her to enroll in the plumbing program at Northern Alberta Institute of Technology (NAIT). There, she was one of three women out of 700 students, and the only woman in the plumbing stream. "I knew I'd be able to make a very good living. And vocational school wasn't expensive. Most of my tuition was covered by a government subsidy," Smith explained.

Before starting classes at NAIT, Smith had to complete 1,500 apprenticeship hours. "I learned in the field," she said. This apprenticeship was followed by two months of classes at NAIT, where she learned what she described as "the science stuff," such as the properties of gases. Smith is a certified Red Seal gas fitter, which allows her to work anywhere in the world—another advantage of being a tradesperson.

PHOTO COURTESY OF AMBER AHMED

HELLO my name is: AMBER AHMED

ALL IN A DAY'S WORK

In Pakistan, where Amber Ahmed grew up, makeup was trendy. "There, the most successful makeup artists earn more than some doctors," Ahmed said. Ahmed attended university in Pakistan. But when she and her husband moved to Montreal in 1998, Ahmed spoke neither English nor French and could not find work.

So Ahmed enrolled in the esthetics program at Gordon Robertson Beauty Academy. "At first, I only spoke Urdu. I learned French and English while taking the course. Some of the students asked me, 'Why are you even taking this class when you can't speak the language?' But I thought, 'You can't just sit there and be a victim. The victim mentality won't get you anywhere,'" she said.

Ahmed learned skills such as waxing, skincare and how to give manicures. She practiced on clients who came to the school for beauty treatments. Ahmed saved every penny she earned from tips, eventually using that money and other savings to open her own salon in 2007.

Amber Esthetics and Makeup Studio specializes in wedding makeup, and many of Ahmed's customers are, like Ahmed, South Asian. When she returned to visit Pakistan in 2020, Ahmed gave free workshops to women and men hoping to pursue careers in esthetics. Here's Ahmed's advice to others who dream of starting their own businesses: "You don't have to have money or even luck. You have to have a goal and determination. Some young people give up too quickly."

THE ROLE OF A MENTOR

Mentors are people with experience who pass on their knowledge to others starting out in the field. Smith's mentor was her grandmother. "She taught me how to fix a lot of stuff," Smith recalled. When Smith was growing up on the family farm, her grandmother did everything the male farmers did, including driving the grain truck. "I grew up thinking women could do anything," Smith said.

Today Smith is a mentor. She recently hired Chelsea Coppel, who is enrolled in the same NAIT plumbing program from which Smith graduated. Coppel is a paid apprentice. Coppel told me that when the two women were working on a job, and Coppel accidentally cracked some threads off a pipe, Smith stayed calm. "Somebody else might have gotten agitated. Carissa is a very good mentor. She's patient, and she takes the time to explain." That ability makes for a good mentor. It's also something Smith's clients appreciate about her.

This new employee is getting on-the-job training from a mentor.
LISA F. YOUNG/SHUTTERSTOCK.COM

IN THE WORKS

Good mentoring pays! Employees who have been successfully mentored tend to get more raises, promotions and greater career opportunities. According to an article published in *Forbes*, 71 percent of Fortune 500 companies have mentoring programs. (Fortune 500 is a list that ranks America's largest companies.)

What's especially interesting is that both the mentor (the person doing the mentoring) and the mentee (the person learning from the mentor) benefit. The mentee learns from the mentor's experience. The mentor feels useful and, because the mentor is often an older person, gets to stay in touch with the younger generation.

Good mentors have a real desire to help others and make themselves available to their mentees. Good mentees ask for help, accept feedback and act on it.

Six

HUMAN RIGHTS AT WORK
EQUITY AND DIVERSITY

THINGS AREN'T ALWAYS FAIR

"That's not fair!"

I bet you've said those words!

Kids are known for their strong sense of justice. You know right away when something isn't fair—for example, getting in trouble for something you didn't do—and you're ready to stand up and say so.

Unfortunately, things aren't always fair in the working world. People from **marginalized communities** have not had the same job opportunities as people from more privileged ones. People have been and continue to be marginalized for just about any reason you can think of—their gender, skin color, ethnicity, religious beliefs, disabilities, sexual orientation, age and more. People who are marginalized may not be hired for a job, and when they do find work, they are often not paid as well, get fewer hours and are less likely to be promoted than, say, an able-bodied white male.

> "Inclusion is not a matter of political correctness. It is the key to growth."
> —Jesse Jackson, American civil rights activist, born 1941

When they first meet principal Roger Rampersad, strangers often assume he is the caretaker of his school. Rampersad is one of the only nonwhite principals working for his school board.

RAMPERSAD

Roger Rampersad is the principal at PACC Adult Education Centre. Born in Trinidad, Rampersad moved to Montreal at the age of three. In elementary school he was the only nonwhite child. He recalls his dad's advice: "You have to work 10 times harder to be considered equal." Even today when Rampersad attends meetings with other principals from his school board, he is one of the few nonwhite persons in the group. When people turn up at his school, they are often surprised to learn that Rampersad is the principal. "In general, anybody who meets me at my school would be more comfortable accepting that I'm the caretaker rather than the principal. That's because it fits a role that belongs to my race," he told me.

When we stereotype members of marginalized communities, we perpetuate inequity, which means lack of equality.

IN THE WORKS

According to research conducted by the Pew Research Center, there are some things women in the working world are better at than men. At right is the list of areas in which women are stronger.

Women are
34 percent
better at working out compromises.

Women are
34 percent
more likely to be honest and ethical.

FIGHTING GENDER INEQUITY

Inequity based on gender is also rampant in the workplace. In the past, some jobs—such as nursing and teaching—were considered "women's work." Other work—such as driving a truck, operating heavy machinery or being in charge of an army—was most commonly done by men. Jobs done mostly by men tend to pay far more than jobs done mostly by women.

This inequity starts as soon as we enter the working world. For many girls, babysitting is their first paid job. Babysitters in my neighborhood are paid $10 an hour. Though boys may also be hired to babysit, their first jobs generally involve physical labor—mowing lawns, painting houses or shoveling snow in winter. These jobs pay, in general, at least twice as much as, and often more than, the hourly babysitting rate.

I bet you're thinking, That's not fair. It isn't.

The situation isn't any better for grown-ups. According to a report issued in 2020 by the University of Ottawa, after graduating from university, Canadian women earn on average 12 percent less than Canadian men. Over time the pay gap widens. In five years after graduation from university, Canadian women earn on average 25 percent less than Canadian men. According to a United Nations report, if things keep going the way they are now, it will take about 164 years to close the pay gap between Canadian women and men.

Women are
25 percent
more likely to stand up for their beliefs.

Women are
30 percent
more likely to provide fair pay and benefits.

Women are
25 percent
better at mentoring.

> **"Don't give up. Believe in yourself. Push hard. Don't be afraid."**
>
> —Marie-Lyne Pelletier, arborist-in-training, born 1991

Around the world and in nearly every industry, far more men than women are in top leadership positions. Women in leadership positions report feeling they have to do more than their male counterparts in order to prove themselves. Does this remind you of the advice Roger Rampersad's dad gave his son?

ALL IN A DAY'S WORK

Marie-Lyne Pelletier was 25 when she decided she wanted to become an arborist, a person who takes care of trees. Most arborists are men. That didn't stop Pelletier. In fact, it made her more interested in the job. "I wanted a job where I could be equal to a man," said Pelletier. After high school, Pelletier worked as a waitress. "I always had the feeling that I was replaceable," Pelletier recalled about her days waitressing. Because she always loved nature, Pelletier's next job was with a landscaping company.

In July 2019 she began working for Émondage Sud-Ouest, a Montreal tree-service company, where she is an arborist-in-training. Pelletier has experienced plenty of sexism on the job, especially when she first joined the team. Some of her male colleagues gave Pelletier a rough time. "When we finish a job, we clean up," she explained. "We put bits of wood in a chipper. When I told one of the guys not to put rocks in the chipper, he said, 'Don't tell me what to do.'" Another time, when Pelletier was about to pick up a giant log, one of her male co-workers told her she wouldn't be able to do it. "But I did it," said Pelletier, who weighs just 100 pounds (45 kilograms)—about the weight of the log she picked up that day.

Pelletier's work is seasonal. She is home with her children between mid-December and the end of March. In tree-cutting season, Pelletier works five to seven days a week, sometimes up to nine hours a day. "I'm incredibly tired afterward. But I'm proud of that too," said Pelletier. Pelletier is saving up for the vocational-training course to become a certified arborist.

HELLO my name is: MARIE-LYNE PELLETIER

PHOTO COURTESY OF MARIE-LYNE PELLETIER

WORKPLACE DISCRIMINATION AGAINST PEOPLE WITH DISABILITIES

Around the world, an estimated one billion people have disabilities, and as many as 80 percent of those people live in poverty. For people with disabilities, discrimination in the workplace takes many forms. Some job candidates with a disability may not even be considered for a job. Some workplaces haven't made the necessary adjustments to accommodate people with disabilities. Not all workplaces, for example, are wheelchair accessible.

Matt Nadeau was born with cerebral palsy, a condition that affected his vision, hand-eye coordination and ability to walk. Matt recently completed a program at a Montreal private vocational school, where he learned to provide technical assistance to computer users. In 2018 he worked at Best Buy, preparing computers for customers. "One of my co-workers told me, 'I've never seen anyone do it so quickly,'" Nadeau said. These days Nadeau works freelance, helping people learn to make better use of their computers. Nadeau says that all his life, he has dealt with others' discomfort with his disability. "When people see a disability, they back off. But when they see what I know and what I can do, they're

Matt Nadeau has not let his disability stop him from pursuing a career in helping people make better use of their computers.
PHOTO COURTESY OF MATT NADEAU

49

like, 'Whoa!'" he told me. Nadeau was hired at Best Buy only for the month before the Christmas rush—and he was not kept on afterward. "I wasn't trained. It wasn't as if it was going to be a full-time job," recalled Nadeau. "We're under-rated." Nadeau has advice for other young people who are marginalized. "Don't be scared of the workforce in general. Having a disability is just part of who we are. We work with what we have. It's what we have," he said.

WORKING FOR CHANGE

People have been working hard—and for many years—to address inequity and lack of diversity (meaning differences between people) in the workplace. In the United States, equal employment opportunity laws were introduced in the 1960s to try to ensure that marginalized groups have a fair chance of being hired and promoted. Much work remains to be done in this area.

But there's some good news. For some companies, equity and diversity are priorities. In the fall of 2020, PepsiCo, a giant food-and-beverage corporation based in New York, pledged to increase gender and racial diversity in its manage-ment by 2025. To build racial diversity, the company has partnered with historically Black colleges and universities to recruit new employees.

The company is no newcomer to the issues of equity and diversity. In 1947 PepsiCo hired an all-Black sales team. Fifteen years later, one of the members of that team, Harvey C. Russell, became the company's vice president, making him the first Black American vice president of a multinational corporation. And from 2006 to 2018, Indra Nooyi led the company as chairperson and CEO. While she was in that job, company revenues increased from $35 billion in 2006 to $63.5 billion in 2017.

While she was working for PepsiCo as chairperson and CEO, Indra Nooyi increased the company's profits from $35 billion in 2006 to $63.5 billion in 2017.

MIKE COPPOLA/GETTY IMAGES

A **mission statement** sums up a company or institution's purpose. PepsiCo's mission statement includes its commitment to equity and diversity. It says, "Our company is strongest when we are a company of opportunity that embraces the full spectrum of humanity. That means building a more diverse, more inclusive workplace."

To truly promote equity and diversity in the workplace, employees must be respected for who they are—not for what they look like, where they came from, their religion, age, disability or whom they love.

IN THE WORKS

According to Statistics Canada, Canadian women earn 87 cents for every dollar made by Canadian men. The situation is even worse for Canadian women who are Black, Indigenous or have disabilities. In Canada, Black women earn 67 cents, Indigenous women, 65 cents, and women with disabilities, 54 cents for every dollar earned by Canadian men. Things are also bad in the United States, where Black women earn 62 cents and Indigenous women 57 cents for every dollar earned by American men. Women there with disabilities earn 72 cents for every dollar earned by men with disabilities.

GETTING ON BOARD

Unfortunately, there has been and continues to be backlash—or negative reaction—to the equity and diversity movement. This backlash usually comes from people who are unwilling to share or give up their privilege. Real equity and diversity will be achieved only when we are all on board. That means that those of us with privilege must use our privilege to support those who are marginalized.

Equity and diversity benefit all of us. Studies indicate that diversity—and respecting **human rights** in the workplace—is good for business. Bringing together people from different backgrounds, with different experiences, boosts productivity and creativity and leads to more effective problem-solving. In a report for the World Economic Forum, Vijay Eswaran noted that a Boston consulting group found that companies with more diverse management teams have 19 percent higher revenues due to innovation.

To create change, companies must begin by learning about equity and diversity. They also need to take a hard look at the data—how many of their employees come from marginalized communities, and if they do, do they have equal opportunity for advancement? If the answer is no, it's time to set targets and recruit diverse employees, and once they are recruited, provide them with the support they need to thrive.

When it comes to achieving true equity and diversity, there is no quick fix. At least for now, the pursuit of true equity and diversity remains a work in progress.

Diversity in the workplace is not a done deal. Companies and institutions still have lots of work to do to ensure equity and diversity.
LUIS ALVAREZ/GETTY IMAGES

Seven

WORK-LIFE BALANCE

IS IT POSSIBLE?

Singer-songwriter Dolly Parton believes there is more to life than work.
TERRY WYATT/GETTY IMAGES

WE CAN'T JUST WORK, WORK, WORK!

If you are lucky (and if, as you learned in chapter four, you are ready for good luck, and if, as you learned in chapter six, you are privileged), you will find a job you enjoy, and you will earn enough money to look after yourself and your loved ones and still have enough time and money left to have some fun.

As we all know, there's more to life than what most of us think of as work.

Take housework. Though some people are hired to clean other people's houses, and your own allowance may be tied to helping around the house, most of us are not paid for cleaning our own houses. There is also volunteer work—community service for which we are not paid but that lets us contribute in a positive, important way to society.

There is also leisure time, which you may decide to spend playing sports, pursuing hobbies, traveling, reading a book or even just flopping down on the couch and watching Netflix.

Most of us do not get paid for tidying up around our own houses, but it's work that needs doing.

IMGORTHAND/GETTY IMAGES

> "I just layered the full-time job of being a mom on top of another full-time job at SPANX and then wondered why I was so exhausted. I started to notice changes in my health and couldn't think as clearly. I feel like this happens to a lot of women."
>
> —Sara Blakely, founder of the undergarments brand SPANX, born 1971

Don't forget friends and family! If you are lucky enough to have kind friends and a supportive family, you will want to do fun stuff with them.

However, many grown-ups talk about how difficult it is to achieve work-life balance.

WHAT IS WORK-LIFE BALANCE ANYHOW?

The expression *work-life balance* is believed to have originated in England during the late 1970s. Women invented the term. They were demanding more flexible working hours as well as maternity leave—they did not want to be penalized for taking time away from their jobs to have babies. They wanted to not only be able to work but also to have a satisfying life outside the workplace.

When you think about it, the term seems to suggest that some kind of perfect balance is possible. Picture a seesaw with a kid at either end who weighs exactly 50 pounds (23 kilograms), not an ounce more. Just as it is difficult to find two kids of exactly the same weight, it is difficult, probably even impossible, to achieve perfect work-life balance. Or perhaps you agree with the late Jack Welch, the former CEO of General Electric, who said, "There's no such thing

as work-life balance. There are work-life choices, and you make them, and they have consequences."

For many people, trying to achieve work-life balance is a never-ending challenge.

Work-life balance seems to matter to some people more than others, and the attempt to balance the two is especially challenging at certain points in our lives.

IT'S GENERATIONAL

Research indicates that baby boomers—people born between 1946 and 1964—have more trouble than younger generations balancing work and life. For many boomers, the seesaw tipped toward work. Because they grew up in the years following World War II, boomers valued stability. Many remained in the same job for years or spent their working lives at one company. They made sacrifices to achieve stability for themselves and their families.

Gen Xers—people born between 1965 and 1980—are the children of boomers. Gen Xers saw how hard their parents worked, how much they sacrificed in terms of family time, and they did not want to do the same. Work-life balance matters more to them than to their parents. At a job interview, typical Gen Xers won't just answer questions. They will ask questions too—about vacation time, maternity and paternity leave, and whether they can work from home. All good questions, of course.

Millennials are the largest population in the North American workforce. Born between 1981 and 1996, they are all over the map when it comes to balancing work and life. Some have an even stronger interest than Gen Xers in life outside of work. And yet, according to a survey by FreshBooks, two-thirds of millennials describe themselves as workaholics.

WORK IN PROGRESS:
Some Things Are More Important Than Work

In June 2020, during the COVID-19 pandemic, Toronto Raptors coach Nick Nurse was supposed to be preparing his team for the start of National Basketball Association games the following month. Nurse thought he'd be putting his energy into work. That changed after the tragic murder of George Floyd, a Minneapolis man who died after being pinned down by police with a knee on his neck. Floyd's death led to protests around the world.

People, many carrying signs that read *Black Lives Matter*, wanted to show they were fed up with racial injustice. In an interview, Nurse explained that during team meetings following Floyd's murder, the subject of basketball rarely came up. "We've really been entrenched in the [George Floyd] issue…making sure everyone's OK, everyone's safe, listening to their ideas and thoughts. As tragic as all these recent events [have been]…there is a historic opportunity to make some lasting change…we all have to take part in that," Nurse said. Standing up for what is right, protesting what is wrong and having important conversations, even when they are difficult—in the workplace and at home—is part of work-life balance.

WORK IN PROGRESS:
Have You Got a Case of Nomophobia?

I don't know about you, but I'd never heard the term **nomophobia** until I wrote this book. Nomophobia is the fear of being without a cell phone. It's not only work-aholics who suffer from this ailment. Teenagers are at risk of nomophobia too, since cell phone use peaks during the teen years. Workaholics also have trouble turning off their cell phones, even on weekends or during holidays. Cell phone addiction can cause insomnia.

Luckily, nomophobia can be treated. Here are four suggestions from coun-selors who treat cell phone dependency:

Hide your phone! Charge your phone in another room. When it's charging, you will be less tempted to check it.

Change your settings to eliminate push notifications.

Build no-cell-phone time into your schedule. Next time you go for a walk with a friend, leave your cell phone at home. How did that make you feel? More anxious or, perhaps, relieved?

Ask yourself tough ques-tions. When you find your-self feeling anxious because you want to check your cell phone, ask yourself, What is really making me anxious? Do I feel bored or sad? Is there something else I could do to make me feel better?

As for your generation, it's too soon to tell. But there's no doubt that living through the COVID-19 pandemic had an effect on your generation's attitudes toward work and life. (Read more about how the pandemic changed the world of work in chapter eight.)

We also know the balance between work and life shifts depending on where we are at in our lives. For example, early in their careers, many people—especially those who are ambitious and hope to rise in their organizations—work very hard to establish themselves. They may feel they have no choice but to sacrifice something—perhaps leisure time or time they might spend with family and friends.

The popularity of home computers and laptops means that more of us can work from home. Our ability to work from home can make it harder to achieve work-life balance.
JUSTIN PAGET/GETTY IMAGES

RAISING A FAMILY

More than anything else, having a family affects work-life balance. Some parents put their careers on hold, staying home in order to look after their children. In the seesaw of work and life, they are choosing—at least for a time—life over work. When I was growing up in the 1960s, only one of my friends' mothers worked outside the home. She was a secretary. Today it is far more common for everyone to have jobs. In couples, will one parent decide to stay home, and for how long? We have all met stay-at-home dads, a choice that has become increasingly common. According to US census data, some seven million American fathers provide regular care for children under the age of 15.

Juggling a job and parenthood is not easy. Despite the fact that, thanks to *feminism*, there is more equality between men and women, research indicates that working moms still get stuck with more house and childcare work than working dads do. The US Bureau of Labor Statistics reported that in 2019, women spent two-and-a-half hours daily doing household chores; men got off easier with just under two hours of daily chore duty.

Research indicates that working moms tend to have it tougher than working dads. In addition to their paying jobs, working moms spend more time doing household chores than their partners (when their partners are male).
10'000 HOURS/GETTY IMAGES

HELLO
my name is:

NANTALI INDONGO

"I don't have work-life balance," says Nantali Indongo. Besides being a member of the Montreal-based hip hop band Nomadic Massive, she is the host of CBC Montreal's arts and culture radio program *The Bridge* and mother of a seven-year-old son. "My son has been going on tour with us since he was five months old. The hardest part is feeling guilt wherever I am, when I feel I am shortchanging something else," Indongo told me.

Indongo never planned to become a musician or journalist. "Music," she says, "was an accident." Indongo grew up in Côte-des-Neiges, a Montreal neighborhood then home to many families like Indongo's—English speakers with roots in the Caribbean. "Hip hop culture was growing," Indongo recalled. "It wasn't just about music—it was about overall artistic expression."

One day Indongo was hanging out with the members of Nomadic Massive,

humming harmonies, when somebody asked, "Can you do that for a show?" Indongo said yes. She began as a backup vocalist. Within a year she was writing songs with the band.

In 2010, Indongo was hired at CBC. "When I was growing up, we had no representation in Canadian arts as Black people," said Indongo. She wanted to change that. Here's Indongo's advice for young people who, like herself, come from marginalized communities: "Don't let what is perceived as your marginalization hold you back. Kids who are marginalized take in, very early in life, that there are perceived designated stations or work they can do in life—and those are too often lesser valued roles in society. But what I'm seeing now is a whole generation of young people who feel they can go on and do whatever they want—pursue a career in any field or make a career."

ADDICTED TO WORK

Have you ever heard the word *workaholic*? It describes a person who is addicted to work, in the same way an alcoholic is addicted to drinking alcohol. Workaholics choose work over life. Sometimes people feel they have no choice, that they must put in long hours of work to succeed. Sometimes people choose work over their personal lives. Researchers call this behavior *compensatory*, meaning that people who do not derive enough satisfaction from their personal lives may decide to put their energy into work instead.

Compensatory hard work is not always a bad thing. As I've already admitted, in my own life I have found that focusing on work steadies me when I am facing life challenges. I forget my problems when I am teaching a class—or writing a book—and for that I have always been grateful.

But working too hard can have negative effects on our health and relationships. It's not fun to live with a workaholic—unless you're a workaholic too. But what, for example, if your parents are so busy working, they can't take time off for a medical checkup or to hang out with you?

Workaholism can also lead to **burnout**—physical, mental and emotional exhaustion that can make it impossible to work. Individuals who work many hours of overtime are at a high risk of burnout. And though companies appreciate hardworking employees, a burned-out employee is bad for business. According to the *Harvard Business Review*, the treatment of burned-out employees costs between $125 and $190 billion a year in American healthcare spending. This hefty price tag includes doctors' bills, hospitalizations, medication and time off for sick days.

Workaholism sometimes leads to burnout, a condition that makes it impossible to keep working.
MICHAEL H/GETTY IMAGES

Working too hard can be deadly. In Japan—a country known for its extreme work culture—the term **karoshi** was coined to describe death caused by overwork. The word refers in particular to deaths that occur in the workplace, generally caused by a stroke or heart attack.

By making us feel useful, work can help give our lives meaning. But if we're not careful and we lose our balance, overwork can threaten our health and even our lives.

Eight

HOW THE COVID-19 PANDEMIC CHANGED WORK

COVID-19 STRIKES

In March 2020, the World Health Organization declared COVID-19 a pandemic. By then the COVID-19 virus had already changed many lives. Some people were sick, some were caring for sick friends and family, some were mourning the deaths of loved ones. Students were adjusting to learning online. We all became expert handwashers and stopped touching our noses and mouths—habits that remain part of our lives.

The pandemic also transformed the world of work.

One of its earliest effects was that it made us appreciate the ***essential workers*** we once took for granted. In an effort to contain the pandemic after it first broke out, most governments shut down nonessential services. For several months, the only stores that remained open were grocery stores and pharmacies. Hospitals, of course, remained open. Public transport had to remain available too. How else could essential workers get to work?

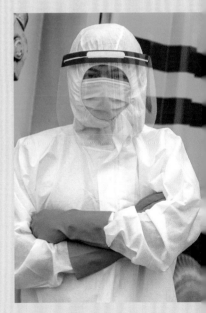

Essential workers continued to do their jobs during the pandemic. Even when they were wearing protective gear, they risked their safety to protect others.
PRAMOTE POLYAMATE/GETTY IMAGES

"Hero's the wrong word," said Cameron Knowlton. "Hero's for the doctors and nurses. I feel like a big helper." Knowlton is a cashier and bagger at a Metro grocery store in Montreal. He began working there in 2018, after graduating from high school. "I was never a fan of books and reading. I wanted to take a break from school and see what the real world was like," he told me.

Knowlton was hard at work during the COVID-19 pandemic when, for several months, grocery stores, considered an essential service, were some of the only businesses to remain open.

"Things were messy," Knowlton said, looking back at the first few months of the pandemic. "I'll admit I was concerned about my health. I went through so much hand sanitizer, the skin on my hands got dry."

Knowlton's parents worried too. Every day when Knowlton arrived home, they sent him straight to the shower.

In April 2020, a month after the pandemic was declared, Knowlton developed flu-like symptoms. Because he did not have a fever, he was not tested for COVID-19. Luckily, within a couple of days he felt better—and was back at the cash register.

For three months during the pandemic, Knowlton's hourly salary increased by two dollars. He would have liked to see that salary increase become permanent. "I think they wanted to make it worth our while during the tough times. But it's not as if everything's normal now."

I interviewed Knowlton on his morning break, nearly five months into the pandemic. I asked him whether customers had been saying thank you more often since the pandemic struck. "No," he answered. "I don't think so."

PHOTO COURTESY OF MONIQUE POLAK

Most of us have always looked up to doctors and nurses. But since the pandemic, our new heroes include hospital orderlies and cleaning staff, bus and taxi or Uber drivers, as well as the employees who stock the shelves and operate the cash registers at grocery stores. During the pandemic, they risked their health to look after us—to get us where we needed to go and keep us healthy and well fed.

In March and April 2020, many Canadian grocery-store chains increased their employees' pay by two dollars an hour. But this increase, referred to in the business world as premium pay, was temporary. By June 2020, grocery chains Loblaws and Metro had phased out the pay increases. In an interview with CBC, Loblaws chairman Galen Weston Jr. explained his company's thinking: "As the economy slowly reopens and Canadians begin to return to work, we believe it is the right time to end the temporary pay premium we introduced at the beginning of the pandemic." Unions were disappointed by this news. Jerry Dias, president of Unifor, a union representing Canadian retail workers, including some at Loblaws and Metro, said, "The pandemic did not make these workers essential and did not create the inequities in retail, it simply exposed them." In other words, grocery-store workers have always been essential—but we took them for granted!

SKYROCKETING UNEMPLOYMENT

Hundreds of millions of people around the world lost their jobs during the pandemic. In the United States, in May 2020, more than 30 million people had applied for unemployment insurance, bringing the country's unemployment rate up to nearly 15 percent, the highest it had been since the **Great Depression**. Many of those laid off from their jobs hoped to be rehired once the pandemic ended. Not surprisingly, people with higher salaries managed better during the pandemic than those with low wages. Poorly paid employees—think servers at restaurants and bars, all of which were closed during the early phases of the pandemic—were hardest hit. According to the Federal Reserve, nearly 40 percent of the poorest households in the United States reported a job loss during the pandemic.

The last time the world experienced record unemployment was during the Great Depression.
FOTOSEARCH/GETTY IMAGES

The situation was similar in Canada. In May 2020, the Canadian unemployment rate soared to 13.7 percent—up from 7.8 percent in March 2020, just before the pandemic was declared. An estimated three million Canadians lost their jobs in March and April 2020, and another 2.5 million Canadian workers' hours were cut during that period.

Governments around the world stepped in to help their citizens. In the United States, Congress and the Federal Reserve introduced rescue measures to help individuals and businesses survive economically. These measures included extended unemployment benefits. The Canadian government

introduced a temporary social security program called the Canada Emergency Response Benefit (CERB) for Canadians who had either lost their jobs or seen their hours drastically reduced during the pandemic.

WORKING FROM HOME

Another effect of the pandemic on the world of work was that those who could do so began working from home. The school where I teach closed on a Friday in March 2020. By Monday I was posting daily YouTube lessons online for my students. The move to online education meant a steep learning curve not only for students but for teachers too!

Though I missed seeing my students in real time, there were things I liked about working from home. For example, I didn't have to drive to work during snowstorms (we still get snowstorms in Montreal in March!). But working from home has its challenges. It is especially hard for people who live in cramped quarters or who have limited internet access. Parents of young children—you may be one of those children, old enough now to be reading this book—also found working from home difficult. Because daycares and schools were closed, these parents not only had to do their jobs,

For many of us, school moved online during the pandemic.
HANANEKO_STUDIO/SHUTTERSTOCK.COM

Parents of young children find working from home especially challenging. Parents need to please their bosses and their kids.
NITAT TERMMEE/GETTY IMAGES

Many essential workers, such as this cashier, are women.
LUIS ALVAREZ/GETTY IMAGES

The pandemic was especially challenging for working women. As Nahla Valji, senior gender adviser at the United Nations, explained in an interview with the *New York Times,* women in every country in the world were already earning and saving less money than men even before the pandemic. With less savings, women who lost their jobs suffered more financially than men did. Women do a lot of essential work. According to reports, two-thirds of workers at grocery-store checkouts and fast-food counters are women. Though these women's work is important, it is underpaid and undervalued.

Around the world, said Valji, women do an average of three times more unpaid work than men. Think cooking, cleaning, household shopping and looking after children and elderly relatives.

But there's some good news! In households where women went to work during the pandemic and their partners stayed home, those partners began doing more household chores and helping more with the kids. According to Alisha Haridasani Gupta, who reports on gender for the *New York Times*, "evidence shows that a temporary shift in the care burden tends to last."

but they also had to look after and help educate their kids. The burden was heaviest on women, who, as research indicates, generally put in more hours on chores and childcare than men do.

It is expected that even after the pandemic, many employees will continue working from home. Many people enjoy the flexibility that comes with working from home, and companies save money when their employees work remotely. Fewer people in a shared office means less money spent on rent and expenses like heating and air-conditioning.

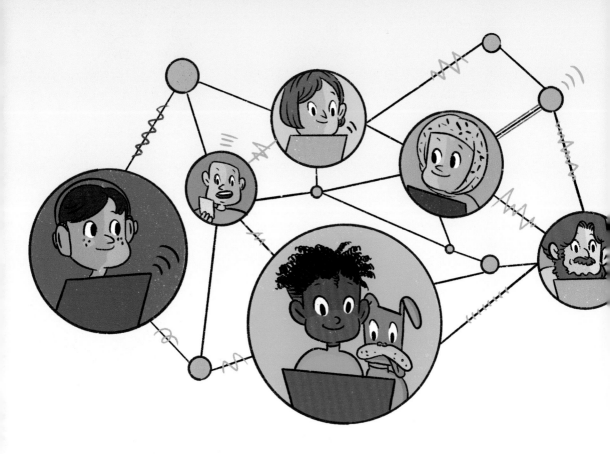

Sometimes even the cat wants to be in on a Zoom call.

Business meetings also changed during the pandemic. You've likely heard of Zoom, one of several online applications that lets us take part in videoconferences. Zoom became so popular during the pandemic that by May 2020 people had started using the word as a verb, as in "I'll Zoom you."

Videoconferencing applications are expected to have a lasting impact on meetings, as well as on business travel. Why go to a meeting downtown when you can take part in the meeting from your dining room? Why travel halfway around the world if you and your colleagues can meet up online? Less business travel will save companies money. It will also benefit the environment by reducing carbon emissions associated with airplane travel.

Yet certain things—intangibles, since we cannot always name or quantify them—risk being lost if everyone works from home.

Chatting with colleagues in the lunchroom is more than an opportunity for social interaction, which many of us enjoy. It provides a chance for co-workers to bounce around ideas.

Though the COVID-19 pandemic brought great upheaval, it gave us a chance to reflect on our lives and consider which elements we want to keep and which elements could use changing. Those elements include the way we approach the world of work.

IN THE WORKS

Zoom meetings are not for everyone. During the COVID-19 pandemic, we heard a lot about something called Zoom fatigue. People working from home who had to attend many Zoom meetings complained they were getting "Zoomed out." Andrew Franklin, an assistant professor of cyberpsychology at Virginia's Norfolk State University, believes virtual interactions can tire us out partly because we try to do too much at once during Zoom meetings listen to whoever is speaking, read on-screen comments and sometimes even check email. "We're engaged in numerous activities, but never fully devoting ourselves to focus on anything in particular," said Franklin.

For others—especially those who dislike in-person meetings—Zoom meetings rule. University of Quebec in Outaouais researcher Claude Normand studies how people with developmental and intellectual disabilities socialize online. She has found that because people on the autism spectrum often have difficulty identifying nonverbal cues—such as when a person clears their throat before saying something—the time lag between speakers on apps like Zoom actually helps.

Nine

GOT A CRYSTAL BALL?

TRYING TO PREDICT THE FUTURE OF WORK

WHAT'S COMING NEXT?

Some people check their horoscopes. They want to know what to expect in the days ahead—and they hope astrology will provide the answers.

There are also **futurists**—consultants paid to make predictions. Futurists' predictions are based on **trends**. Of course, like astrologers, futurists don't always get it right. But that doesn't stop them—or us—from trying to imagine the future.

One of many areas futurists look at is the world of work.

Vivek Wadhwa is a futurist. A fellow at Harvard Law School, Wadhwa is also the co-author of *The Driver in the Driverless Car: How Our Technology Choices Will Create the Future*. Wadhwa lives in Silicon Valley, an area of California that is home to many major technology companies, including Apple and Google.

Vivek Wadhwa (left) makes a living predicting what our world will look like in the future.

THEO WARGO/GETTY IMAGES

IN THE WORKS

In an article in *Medium*, journalist Teodor Teofilov lists 42 new jobs he predicts will exist by 2050. Here are some of the most intriguing examples:

- **Digital detective**—investigates online data and helps companies use that information to increase profits
- **Fitness commitment counselor**—keeps clients motivated to exercise
- **Financial wellness coach**—helps people manage their online bank accounts
- **Joy adjutant**—brings more happiness to customers' lives
- **Virtual-store guide**—makes online shopping easier
- **Walker/talker**—walks with seniors mobile enough to go for walks and chats with them. Teofilov believes this job will suit people who enjoying hearing stories.

These drones were used in Chile during the COVID-19 lockdown to safely deliver food and medicine to seniors.

MARCELO HERNANDEZ/GETTY IMAGES

When futurists try to predict what will be going on in the world of work in 2050, they consider current and future trends, such as the increasing use of robotics and AI (artificial intelligence), the continued growth of what is known as the gig economy (in which workers choose or accept gigs over traditional jobs), an aging population and the need to protect the environment.

ROBOTS FOR HIRE

Of all the trends futurists identify, the use of robotics and AI is expected to have the greatest impact on the world of work. According to the World Economic Forum, by the year 2025 half of all work tasks will be able to be done by machines. "Millions of jobs in every industry will be wiped out," Wadhwa said. He predicts that by 2025 we'll have driverless vehicles, leaving truck and taxi drivers out of work.

People whose jobs involve repetitive motion, such as assembly-line workers and grocery-store cashiers, are already being replaced by technology.

Even pilots may find themselves unemployed, replaced by unpiloted aircraft. As for the stuff we order online, Wadhwa believes that soon packages will be delivered to your doorstep by ***drones***. Doctors' jobs will change too. Wadhwa expects

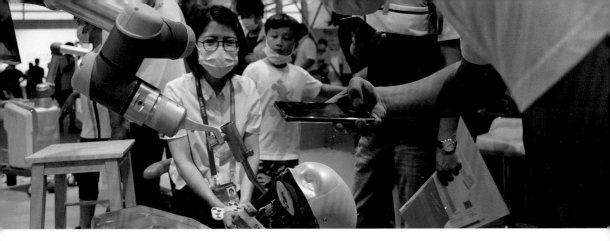

that AI will be used to diagnose diseases and that robots will be able to perform many surgeries. Except when dealing with the most complicated cases, medical health professionals will meet with patients remotely.

Wadhwa worries the working world is not ready for the changes coming our way—mass unemployment and the need to reinvent ourselves. He predicts social turmoil. "There will be anger and resentment," Wadhwa said.

But Wadhwa also believes our resilience and ability to learn will help us adapt. Continuous technological advances will mean that careers of the future will likely last just 5 to 10 years. Wadhwa's advice to young people? "Learn how to be learning all the time."

A GIG'S A JOB TOO

Have you heard the word *gig*? You might take a gig babysitting a neighbor's kid on Sunday mornings. A musician has a gig at a local club. Both you and the musician manage your own work schedules. You can sleep in on Sunday morning—and send your cousin over to the neighbors instead.

Gigs are temporary and sometimes on contract. Gig work, also known as working freelance, exists in most industries. Someone may get a gig painting a house or designing a computer program. On the downside, gig workers lack job security and do not have unions to support them.

Students watch as a robot performs surgery.
LINTAO ZHANG/GETTY IMAGES

House painting is an example of a gig. These house painters may have other gigs or jobs.
AVALON_STUDIO/GETTY IMAGES

On the upside, gig workers are independent, have flexibility and do not feel tied down by a job.

According to a study in 2017, 20 to 30 percent of the Canadian workforce at that time consisted of ***nontraditional workers***—people who did not have regular full-time jobs. Many workers in the gig economy work part-time or, thanks to the internet, virtually. For some people, gigs are a second job, a way to earn extra income.

The gig economy arose in part because businesses wanted to cut costs. Gig workers are cheaper than regular full-time employees whose benefits include health insurance, pensions and vacation pay. Gig work appeals to many young people by giving them more free time when they want it and a better work-life balance.

Futurists predict that by the year 2050, five billion of the world's six billion workers will be gig workers. But they warn that society must find ways to protect workers in the gig economy.

PHOTO COURTESY OF MEGHAN KERR

ALL IN A DAY'S WORK

Meghan Kerr is chief lifeguard at the swimming pool at Montreal's Monkland Tennis Club. But she has other gigs. She cofounded a production company and writes texts for videos. Kerr has been lifeguarding since she was 15. In fact, she learned to swim at the pool she now works at.

Kerr studied professional theater at Dawson College. Soon after the pandemic struck, she founded Endurance Films with friends from the theater program. "We called it Endurance because on the first day of theater school, one of our teachers showed us a photo of Sir Ernest Shackleton's boat *Endurance* and told us, 'To make it in this industry, you need endurance.'"

Kerr never expected to write professionally. As a child she was diagnosed with **dyslexia**, **dysgraphia** and **ADHD** (attention-deficit/hyperactivity disorder). "When I was in grade six, my decoding and spelling were at the grade-three level," she said. Professional support changed Kerr's life. "I gained confidence, and the ability to advocate for myself," she said. Today Kerr is an ambassador for the Montreal Centre for Learning Disabilities. The center even hired Kerr's production company to make a promotional video. Kerr, who is a member of the LGBTQ+ community, says she became interested in TV and movies because she didn't see herself or her friends represented on-screen. "I want to help facilitate the telling of stories of people who are marginalized," she said.

GETTING OLDER AND LIVING LONGER

The steadily increasing number of senior citizens will also affect the future of work. Thanks to medical advances, people are living longer. According to a United Nations study, by 2050 one in six people—or 16 percent of the world's population—will be over age 65. Compare that to 2018, when only 9 percent of the world's population was that old. Seniors will need more help, whether they live on their own, with family or in seniors' residences. Some of that help will come from robots. "Robots will be friends and companions," Wadhwa said. But even with robots pitching in, we can expect more jobs in geriatrics, which is medical care for the seniors' sector.

WORKING TO SAVE THE PLANET

We don't need a futurist to tell us Earth is in big trouble. In 2021 the United Nations Intergovernmental Panel on Climate Change (IPCC) warned that if things don't change, we are in for environmental disaster. Among the IPCC's recommendations are the restoration of forests, since trees absorb and store carbon dioxide, then release oxygen into the atmosphere, and more efficient food production.

This engineer has a green job, supervising the production of solar panels.
ALVAREZ/GETTY IMAGES

This means that by 2050 we can expect a huge demand for green jobs—ones that contribute to the sustainability of the environment. Electric cars may not need drivers, but they will need electricians to service them. Scientists and engineers need to continue investigating alternative fuels such as bioenergy and hydrogen. Solar photovoltaic installers will be busy putting solar panels on rooftops and other structures. And geoscientists who study Earth's

composition will help environmental scientists clean up and preserve our planet.

Huge advances in solar and battery-storage technology are expected by 2030. "The cost of clean energy will drop by 80 to 90 percent. We'll be moving to a clean economy," said Wadhwa. Millions of jobs will be created around our use of solar energy.

Vertical farming will let us grow more food in less space and use less water than traditional farming. Pesticide-free produce is grown without soil in stacked racks. Big cities like Tokyo and New York are already experimenting with vertical farming. Urban farming in controlled environments such as vertical farms and indoor or rooftop farms would also help reduce carbon emissions currently associated with the transport of food.

WORK IN PROGRESS
Tokyo Farms Vertically

Japan imports 60 percent of its food. That may be why it pioneered vertical farming. The first vertical farms in Japan were created in the 1970s, but vertical farming took off in 2010, when energy-saving LED lights became available (making vertical farming less expensive) and the Japanese government began supporting this innovative farming method.

Shinji Inada, president of Spread, the Japanese company that operates the country's largest vertical farms, started out as a vegetable trader. He opened his first vertical farm in Kameoka in 2007. There, 300 heads of lettuce can be grown annually in 10.8 square feet (one square meter), compared to 5 in a traditional farm. Each head of lettuce needs only 3.7 fluid ounces (110 milliliters) of water—1 percent of the amount of water needed for a traditionally grown head of lettuce. Inada hopes to expand his vertical farming business beyond Japan. "We are targeting countries where fresh vegetables cannot be produced because of scarce water, extremely low temperatures or other natural conditions," he said.

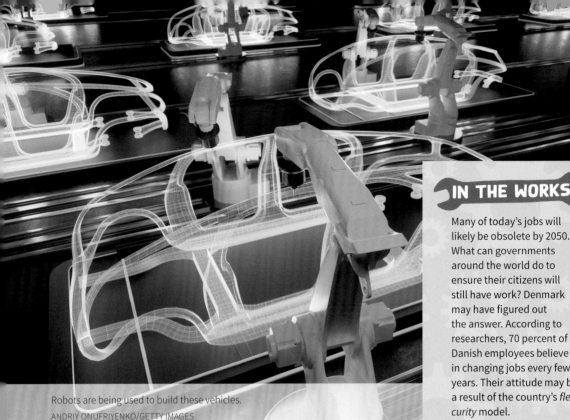

Robots are being used to build these vehicles.
ANDRIY ONUFRIYENKO/GETTY IMAGES

A FEW MORE THINGS I WANT TO SAY BEFORE I END THIS BOOK

Perhaps now when someone asks, "What do you want to be when you grow up?" you will have a new perspective. I used to think the answer mattered, but now I'm not so sure it does. Maybe you know exactly what kind of work you want to do, or maybe you have no idea. Maybe you'll end up doing exactly what you've got planned. Maybe chance events will lead you in another direction.

I think what matters most is that, along the way, you feel good about yourself and the work you do, that no matter the challenges you face, no matter how hard you work, you make time for yourself and those you love.

And that while you're at it, you help to make our world a little better.

So what are you waiting for? Get to work!

Glossary

ADHD (attention-deficit/hyperactivity disorder)—a mental health disorder that makes concentrating on a single task difficult

aptitude tests—common in the 1980s, tests that attempted to match personality traits with existing jobs

burnout—a state of physical, mental and emotional exhaustion that can eventually make it impossible to work

career—a long-term profession or field, often requiring a certain level of education or training

caste system—a social structure, believed to date back to 1000 BC, that divides people into classes based on heredity and determines the kind of work a Hindu child living in India will do when he or she is old enough to work

child labor—work that exploits children, such as forcing them to work when they are too young and/or placing them in harmful or dangerous working conditions

child trafficking—a serious crime by which children are recruited, kidnapped and forced to work as slaves

dementia—loss of memory as well as problem-solving and language skills, often caused by Alzheimer's disease

developed world—countries with widespread development of different kinds of industries

developing world—countries with low- to middle-income economies and less developed industries

diversity—people of different races and cultures in a group or business

drones—unpiloted aircraft

dysgraphia—a brain-based learning disability that affects writing and fine motor skills

dyslexia—a brain-based learning disability that can affect reading, writing and spelling skills

equity—the quality of being fair or just in how we treat others. In the workplace it means ensuring everyone is given access to resources and opportunities to succeed.

essential workers—critical workers in the public or private sectors, such as grocery-store cashiers, bus drivers, health providers and so on

exploitation—taking advantage of a person or a group of people

feminism—a movement that advocates for men and women to have equal rights

futurists—consultants paid to made predictions based on current trends

gig economy—a market in which workers choose or accept gigs (flexible, temporary or freelance work) over traditional jobs

Great Depression—a worldwide economic depression that lasted from 1929 until 1933

happenstance—a random or chance event

homework—assignments students are asked to complete outside of class

human rights—rights that belong to every person, including the rights to equality, freedom and personal security

Industrial Revolution—the period of transition in the 18th to 19th centuries in Europe and North America from a mostly farm-based and handicraft economy to a machine driven one, as new manufacturing processes were introduced

internship—a period of on-the-job training, known in Quebec as a stage, that can be paid or unpaid

job—a task or regular activity that requires physical and mental energy and that is generally performed in exchange for payment; can be full- or part-time, short- or long-term, and is often based on a contract between an employer and a worker

karoshi—a Japanese term to describe death caused by overwork

labor movement—a political movement that arose to improve people's working conditions and living standards

marginalized communities—populations of people who are discriminated against or excluded on the basis of such factors as gender, skin color, ethnicity, religious beliefs, disabilities, sexual orientation and age

mentors—experienced people who provide guidance to those who are less experienced or just starting out in a certain field

minimum wage—the lowest wage permitted by law

mission statement—a summary of a company's or institution's purpose

nomophobia—the fear of being without a cell phone

nontraditional workers—workers who do not have regular, full-time jobs
   (see *gig economy*)

professions—jobs that require specialized university training—for example, architect, engineer or doctor

radioactivity—the property of tiny particles in some objects to emit energy or tinier particles

sex trade—activities involved in the sale of sex, such as prostitution

slave labor—hard work for which people are paid little or nothing

soft skills—sometimes called *people skills*, they include common sense, the ability to deal with others, and flexibility

sweatshops—factories with poor working conditions; these factories often rely on child labor

trade unions—legal associations of workers formed to secure better working conditions and higher pay for their members; known in the United States as *labor unions*

trends—changes or developments in a particular direction, such as the trend toward working from home

unskilled labor—work that requires no special training

vocational schools—schools that provide technical training for jobs, often in the trades; also known as *trade schools*

volunteer work—unpaid work, usually connected with helping others

work—activity involving physical or mental effort, meant to achieve a purpose

workaholics—people who choose to work a lot and whose jobs interfere with their ability to enjoy life fully

working remotely—working outside of a traditional office, such as from home, a shared workspace or even a coffee shop!

work-life balance—the balance between working hard and having a satisfying life outside of work

Resources

Bolles, Richard N., and Carol Christen. *What Color Is Your Parachute? for Teens: Discover Yourself, Design Your Future, and Plan for Your Dream Job*. Berkeley, CA: Ten Speed Press, 2015.

*A career guide for teens, based on a book with a similar title written by Richard N. Bolles for adults

Olsen, Sylvia, and Cate May Burton. *Growing Up Elizabeth May: The Making of an Activist*. Victoria, BC: Orca Book Publishers, 2021.

*This inspiring biography of Canadian politician and environmental activist Elizabeth May provides insight into a career in public service.

Pawlewski, Sarah. *The Graphic Guide to Planning Your Future*. New York: DK Children, 2015.

*A guide that introduces kids to some 400 different careers

Penn, Maya S. *You Got This! Unleash Your Awesomeness, Find Your Path, and Change Your World*. New York: Simon & Schuster, 2016.

*Teen entrepreneur and activist shares her own inspiring story

Reynolds, Jason. *The Boy in the Black Suit*. New York: Atheneum, 2015.

*A YA (young adult) novel in which Matt, the protagonist, has an unusual job— he works in a funeral parlor

Saeed, Aisha. *Amal Unbound*. New York: Penguin Random House, 2018.

*A novel in which we meet Amal, a Pakistani girl forced into slavery to pay off her family's debts

Saujani, Reshma. *Girls Who Code: Learn to Code and Change the World*. New York: Puffin, 2018.

*Reshma Saujani is the founder of the Girls Who Code organization. This book tells the stories of girls and women who work with computers at places like NASA and Pixar.

Seuss, Dr. *Oh, the Places You'll Go.* New York: Penguin Random House, 1990.
    *A fun but profound book about trying and failing and then trying again

Wadhwa, Vivek, and Alex Salkever. *The Driver in the Driverless Car: How Our Technology Choices Will Create the Future.* Oakland, CA: Berrett-Koehler, 2017.
    *This book about jobs of the future is written for adults, but younger strong readers will also enjoy it.

Weissman, Elissa Brent, Kwame Alexander, Tom Angleberger and others. *Our Story Begins: Your Favorite Authors and Illustrators Share Fun, Inspiring, and Occasionally Ridiculous Things They Wrote and Drew as Kids.* New York: Atheneum, 2017.
    *This collection of childhood works by well-known children's authors and illustrators provides great examples of young talent.

White, E.B. *The Trumpet of the Swan.* New York: Harper and Row, 1970.
    *A novel about a swan who gets through life without a voice. A powerful story about overcoming handicaps.

Wishinsky, Frieda, and Elizabeth MacLeod. *How to Become an Accidental Genius.* Victoria, BC: Orca Book Publishers, 2019.
    *A book about inventors and how they came up with their inventions

Acknowledgments

The idea for this book hatched at my dining room table. My friend Ruth Linka, associate publisher at Orca, and I were batting around ideas. Thanks, Ruth, for believing in this one from the start. Thanks to the team at Orca for bringing this project to life. Special thanks to editor Kirstie Hudson for her keen eye, insightful comments and steadfast encouragement. Thanks to Orca editorial assistant Georgia Bradburne for looking after all the details. Thanks to Suharu Ogawa for her fun and thought-provoking illustrations. Thanks to the many people—young and older—who agreed to be interviewed. Finally, thanks to Guy, who works super hard but knows when to say, "Put the computer on sleep. It's time for a walk."

Index

*Page numbers in **bold** indicate an image caption.*

JOHN FREDERICKS

MONIQUE POLAK is the author of more than 30 books for young people. She is a three-time winner of the Quebec Writers' Federation Prize for Children's and YA Literature for her novels *Hate Mail*, *What World is Left* and *Room for One More*. In addition to teaching at Marianopolis College in Montreal, Monique is a freelance journalist whose work has appeared in *Maclean's Magazine*, the *Montreal Gazette* and other Postmedia newspapers. She is also a columnist on ICI Radio-Canada's *Plus on est de fous, plus on lit!* In 2016 Monique was the CBC/Quebec Writers' Federation inaugural writer-in-residence. Monique lives in Montreal.

THE MORE YOU KNOW
THE MORE YOU GROW

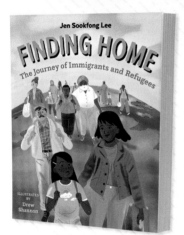

FINDING HOME
The Journey of Immigrants and Refugees
Jen Sookfong Lee
ILLUSTRATED BY Drew Shannon

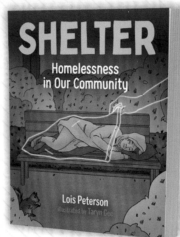

SHELTER
Homelessness in Our Community
Lois Peterson
illustrated by Taryn Gee

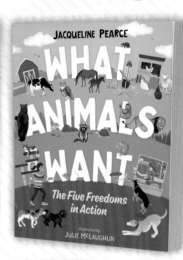

JACQUELINE PEARCE
WHAT ANIMALS WANT
The Five Freedoms in Action
Illustrated by JULIE McLAUGHLIN

SAVE NATURAL HABITATS!!

Megan Clendenan
illustrated by Julie McLaughlin
Fresh Air, Clean Water
Our Right to a Healthy Environment

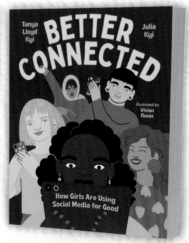

Tanya Lloyd Kyi
Julia Kyi
BETTER CONNECTED
illustrated by Vivian Rosas
How Girls Are Using Social Media for Good

WHAT'S THE BIG IDEA?

The **Orca Think** series introduces us to the issues making headlines in the world today. It encourages us to question, connect and take action for a better future. With those tools we can all become better citizens. Now that's smart thinking!